Hörthemen
Aural and Vocabulary Comprehension

Leaving Certificate Ordinary and Higher Levels

James Hayes

CJ Fallon
ESTABLISHED 1895

Published by
CJ Fallon
Ground Floor – Block B
Liffey Valley Office Campus
Dublin 22

ISBN 978-0-7144-1730-1

First Edition April 2010
This Reprint September 2020

Printed in Ireland by
W&G Baird Limited
Caulside Drive
Antrim BT41 2RS

Contents

Ordinary Level

Higher Level

Hörthemen

Ordinary Level

Aural Comprehension

Wortschatz

das Alter – *old age*
die Rente – *pension*
der Rentner/die Rentnerin – *pensioner*
Senioren – *senior citizens*
das Seniorenheim – *old folks home*
die Gesellschaft – *company/society*
das Enkelkind (-er) – *grandchild*
die Einsamkeit – *loneliness*
die Isolierung – *isolation*
Probleme der Gesundheit – *health problems*
besuchen – *to visit*
pensioniert – *retired*
im Ruhestand sein – *to be retired*
einkaufen gehen – *to go shopping*
sauber machen – *to clean*
reden mit ihnen – *to talk to them*
ihnen Gesellschaft leisten – *to keep them company*

Test 1

German – Ordinary Level
LISTENING COMPREHENSION

First Part   CD1 Track 2

The interview will be played **three** times – the second time with pauses.

1. Why is Laura so frustrated? Explain giving **two** details.

    _____

    _____

2. Michael describes a particular scheme:
    (i)   What is the title of the scheme?

    _____

(ii) Explain how the scheme works, mentioning **two** details.

_____

_____

3. What kind of help does Michael's landlord need?
   Explain why, giving **three** details.

_____

_____

_____

4. Why could Michael not move in immediately?

_____

_____

_____

5. At the end of the conversation, Laura and Michael both agree that
   the scheme is an excellent one. Mention any **two** advantages they see in it.

_____

_____

Second Part

CD1 Track 3

You will now hear a telephone conversation **three** times. The receptionist takes a message
from the caller.

1. What problem is the caller concerned about? Give details.

_____

_____

_____

2. The caller is annoyed. Give **two** details to show this.

_____

_____

3. What are the name and the phone number of the caller?

   Name: _____

   Phone Number: _____

4. The phonecall is to:
(a) a bank.
(b) a retirement home.
(c) a hospital.
(d) a hotel.

Indicate your answer by putting **a**, **b**, **c** or **d** in the box provided. ☐

Third Part

CD1 Track 4

You will now hear a conversation between two people. The dialogue will be played **three** times, with a pause after each playing. Answer in English.

1. (i) Why is Frau Adam annoyed with Herr Lehmann?

_____

_____

_____

   (ii) Where is Herr Lehmann working?

_____

_____

_____

2. Why does Frau Adam say that he has a bad attitude (*Einstellung*)?

_____

_____

_____

_____

3. Mention **two** things which Herr Lehmann thinks are unfair about his situation.

_____

_____

4. At the end of the conversation, Herr Lehmann decides:
(a) to leave the job.
(b) to join the army.
(c) to look for alternative work.
(d) to continue working in his present job.

Indicate your answer by putting **a**, **b**, **c** or **d** in the box provided. ☐

Fourth Part

You will now hear **four** news items taken from the radio, followed by the weather forecast. The news will be played **three** times; the first time right through, then in five segments with pauses, and finally right through again.

(Item 1)   CD1 Track 5

1. (i)   How much money was stolen from the patient?

_____

(ii) How did the employee steal the money?

_____

_____

(Item 2)   CD1 Track 6

2. (i)   How long can 65-year-olds expect to live?

_____

(ii) Mention **one** reason why wealthier pensioners live longer than those less well off.

_____

(Item 3)   CD1 Track 7

3. (i)   According to the EU survey, what are the **two** things
            of most concern to pensioners?

_____

_____

(ii) What percentage of those asked agreed?

_____

_____

(Item 4)   CD1 Track 8

4. (i)   Where did the attack described here take place?

_____

_____

(ii) What did the two young men steal?

_____

_____

_____

_____

(Item 5)

CD1 Track 9

5. Weather Forecast
   What type of weather is forecast:
   (i) for today?

   _____

   _____

   (ii) for the weekend?

   _____

   _____

Wortschatz

der Ausländer(-) – *foreigner(s)*
der Immigrant(-en) – *immigrant(s)*
Arbeit suchen – *to look for work*
der Flüchtling(-e) – *refugee(s)*
der Rassismus – *racism*
flüchten – *to flee*
die Hautfarbe – *skin colour*
die Heimat – *homeland*
das Ausland – *abroad*
die Sprache – *language*
die Toleranz – *tolerance*
die Qualifikation(-en) – *qualification(s)*
die Sozialhilfe – *social welfare*
das Vorurteil(-e) – *prejudice*
die Kultur(-en) – *culture(s)*
integriert werden – *to become integrated*
der Unterschied(e) – *difference*
leben und leben lassen – *to live and let live*
akzeptieren – *to accept*
die Festung Europa – *Fortress Europe*

Test 2

German – Ordinary Level
LISTENING COMPREHENSION

First Part   CD1 Track 12

The interview will be played **three** times: the second time with pauses.

1. (i)   Where does Herr Özkan work? Give details.

    _____

    _____

    (ii) How long has he been living in Germany?

    _____

2. What was the extent of Herr Özkan's knowledge of German when he first arrived in Germany?

_____

_____

3. (i) What problems did Herr Özkan face when he started school?

_____

(ii) Why did he not wish to go to college? Give **two** details.

_____

_____

4. (i) What did Herr Özkan do immediately after he left school?

_____

_____

(ii) What other jobs did he do before he settled into his current job? Give details.

_____

_____

_____

5. What are Herr Özkan's plans for the future? Mention **two** details.

_____

_____

Second Part

CD1 Track 13

You will now hear a telephone conversation **three** times. The secretary takes a message from the caller.

1. What problem is the caller concerned about? Give details.

_____

_____

_____

2. The caller is dissatisfied. Give **two** details to show this.

_____

_____

3. What are the name and the phone number of the caller?

   Name: _____

   Phone Number: _____

4. The phonecall is to:
   (a) a university.
   (b) a secondary school.
   (c) a primary school.
   (d) a factory.

   Indicate your answer by putting **a**, **b**, **c** or **d** in the box provided. ☐

Third Part   CD1 Track 14

You will now hear a conversation between two people. The dialogue will be played **three** times, with a pause after each playing. Answer in English.

1. (i) Why did Fatima skip school today?

   _____

   _____

   (ii) What is she compelled to wear?

   _____

   _____

2. Why does Bastian say about those who make fun of her?

   _____

   _____

3. Mention any **two** suggestions made by Bastian.

   _____

   _____

4. At the end of the conversation, Fatima decides:
   (a) to talk to the class teacher.
   (b) to leave school.
   (c) to do what her parents say.
   (d) to run away from home.

   Indicate your answer by putting **a**, **b**, **c** or **d** in the box provided. ☐

Fourth Part

You will now hear **four** news items taken from the radio, followed by the weather forecast. The news will be played **three** times; the first time right through, then in five segments with pauses, and finally right through again.

(Item 1)   `CD1 Track 15`

1. (i) Where did the incident reported here happen? Mention **two** details.

_____

_____

(ii) How many people were injured?

_____

_____

(Item 2)   `CD1 Track 16`

2. (i) Where was the family from?

_____

_____

(ii) How much money was stolen?

_____

_____

(Item 3)   `CD1 Track 17`

3. (i) How many people of German origin (*Aussiedler*) applied to move to Germany the previous year?

_____

_____

(ii) What percentage of applicants failed the German test?

_____

_____

(Item 4)   `CD1 Track 18`

4. (i) What is causing concern to the Federal government? Mention **one** detail.

_____

(ii) What percentage of those caught are foreigners?

_____

_____

CD1 Track 19

5. Weather Forecast

   (i)   What type of weather is expected for today? Give **two** details.

_____

_____

   (ii) What kind of weather is forecast for the weekend? Give **two** details.

_____

_____

Revision 1

1. List the **ten** numbers mentioned on the CD.

_____   _____

_____   _____

_____   _____

_____   _____

_____   _____

2. Food.
   Translate the **ten** food items mentioned on the CD.

_____   _____

_____   _____

_____   _____

_____   _____

_____   _____

3. Scenery.
   Name the **ten** types of scenery mentioned on the CD.

_____   _____

_____   _____

_____   _____

_____   _____

_____   _____

4. Germany.
   List the **ten** geographical items mentioned on the CD.

_____   _____

_____   _____

_____   _____

_____   _____

_____   _____

5. List the **five** names spelled out on the CD.

_____

_____

_____

_____

_____

Wortschatz

der Austausch – *exchange*
der/die Austauschpartner/-in – *exchange partner*
Deutschkenntnisse (pl.) – *knowledge of German*
aufbessern – *to improve*
die Alltagssprache – *everyday language*
auskommen mit (+ Dat.) – *to get on with*
der Deutschkurs(e) – *German course(s)*
bei einer Familie – *with a family*
Sitten und Gebräuche kennen lernen – *to get to know customs and traditions*
die gesprochene Sprache – *the spoken language*
die Redewendung(-en) – *phrases/idioms*
die Einheimischen – *the natives*
Dialekt(e) – *dialect*
seine Horizonte erweitern – *to broaden one's horizons*
andere Länder, andere Sitten – *different countries/different customs*
die Globalisierung – *globalisation*
eine andere Mentalität – *a different mentality*

Test 3

German – Ordinary Level

LISTENING COMPREHENSION

First Part   CD1 Track 22

Listen to the CD. The interview will be played **three** times – the second time with pauses.

1. (i)   When did Detlef Soitzek start the High Seas High School project in Germany?

    _____

    (ii) What is his role in the project?

    _____

    _____

2. (i) How long does the project last each year?

_____

_____

(ii) Who else is on board the ship? Give **two** details.

_____

_____

3. (i) Mention **four** subjects taught on board ship.

_____

_____

_____

_____

(ii) Give **one** example of a project that the pupils get involved in on dry land.

_____

4. Mention **one** of the regular chores to be done on the _Thor Heyerdahl_.

_____

5. What proves that the students have learned a lot about sailing during the voyage? Give details.

_____

_____

_____

Second Part

CD1 Track 23

You will now hear a telephone conversation **three** times. The secretary takes a message from the caller.

1. The caller had made a reservation. What exactly had he reserved? Give **two** details.

_____

_____

2. Why is the caller dissatisfied? Give **two** details.

_____

_____

3. What are the surname and the phone number of the caller?

Name: _____

Phone Number: _____

4. The phonecall is to:
   (a) a bank.
   (b) a youth hostel.
   (c) a travel agency.
   (d) a restaurant.

   Indicate your answer by putting **a, b, c** or **d** in the box provided. ☐

Third Part

CD1 Track 24

You will now hear a conversation between two people. The dialogue will be played **three** times, with a pause after each playing. Answer in English.

1. Ingo and Salome have different plans for their school holidays. What are they?

   Ingo: _____

   _____

   Salome: _____

   _____

2. Why is Salome not happy with her holiday arrangements. Mention **three** reasons.

   _____

   _____

   _____

3. What does Ingo suggest Salome should do to improve her holiday situation?

   _____

   _____

4. What holiday plans has Salome for next year?
   (a) She hopes to travel somewhere with Ingo.
   (b) She wants to go to Turkey with a classmate.
   (c) She will return to Denmark without her brother.
   (d) She intends to go to Greece.

   Indicate your answer by putting **a, b, c** or **d** in the box provided. ☐

Fourth Part

You will now hear **four** news items taken from the radio, followed by the weather forecast. The news will be played **three** times; the first time right through, then in five segments with pauses, and finally right through again.

(Item 1)   CD1 Track 25

1. (i) Who was killed in the accident?

_____

_____

   (ii) Give details of when the accident happened.

_____

_____

(Item 2)   CD1 Track 26

2. (i) How many journalists died while reporting last year?

_____

_____

   (ii) What were the main causes of death? Mention any **two**.

_____

_____

(Item 3)   CD1 Track 27

3. Give details of the kidnapping in Columbia. (Who? By whom?)

_____

_____

(Item 4)   CD1 Track 28

4. (i) What is the cause of the traffic problems at this time?

_____

_____

   (ii) Where are the problems at their worst? Give **two** details.

_____

_____

_____

(Item 5)

5. Weather Forecast

What type of weather is forecast:

(i) for today? Give any **two** details.

_____

_____

(ii) for the next few days? Give any **two** details.

_____

_____

Wortschatz

das Auto(s) – *car*
der Zug (Züge) – *train*
die Bahn – *rail*
die Straßenbahn – *tram*
das Fahrrad (-räder) – *bicycle*
der/ die Fahrer/-in – *driver*
der Führerschein – *licence*
die Versicherung – *insurance*
die Erfahrung – *experience*
das Benzin – *petrol*
die Gefahr(-en) – *danger*
gefährlich – *dangerous*
die Geschwindigkeit – *speed*
rasen – *to speed*
zu schnelles Fahren – *speeding*
(die) Trunkenheit am Steuer – *drink driving*
öffentliche Verkehrsmittel (pl.) – *public (means of) transport*
der Unfall(-fälle) – *accident*
der Verkehr – *traffic*
der Stau – *traffic-jam*
praktisch – *convenient*
das Warten – *waiting*
die Unkosten – *costs*
die Umwelt – *the environment*
angeben – *to show-off*
vorschlagen – *to suggest*

Test 4

German – Ordinary Level

LISTENING COMPREHENSION

First Part

CD1 Track 32

The interview will be played **three** times – the second time with pauses.

1. (i)   How long has Jens been a taxi-driver?

    (ii) Driving a taxi is a sideline for Jens. Why does he work as a taxi driver?
          Give **one** reason.

2. Mention any **two** conditions (apart from passing a medical test) that one must fulfil
    in order to obtain a licence to drive a taxi.

3. Mention any **one** of the tests Jens had to undergo during his medical examination.

4. (i)   Jens also had to pass both written and oral examinations. What was tested in
          these examinations? Mention any **two** details (one oral and one written).

    (ii) How much did Jens have to pay?

5. (i)   What aspects of the work appeal to Jens? Mention **two** details.

    (ii) Mention any **two** aspects that he does not enjoy.

Second Part

CD1 Track 33

You will now hear a telephone conversation **three** times. The secretary takes a message
from the caller.

1. What problem is the caller concerned about? Give details.

2. What are the name and the phone number of the caller?

    Name:

    Phone Number:

3. What is (i) the make and (ii) the registration number of the car?

    Make: _____

    Registration Number: _____

4. The caller is calling from a:
    (a) hotel.
    (b) car.
    (c) phone booth.
    (d) neighbour's house.

    Indicate your answer by putting **a, b, c** or **d** in the box provided. ☐

Third Part

CD1 Track 34

You will now hear a conversation between two people. The dialogue will be played **three** times, with a pause after each playing. Answer in English.

1. (i)   Who came up with the idea of car sharing?

        _____

    (ii) Why did they choose the particular persons to share with?

        _____

        _____

2. Why is Maike in favour of car sharing? Give **two** reasons.

    _____

    _____

3. Mention **two** reasons why Sven is particularly annoyed.

    _____

    _____

4. Maike wants to:
    (a) stop sharing the car immediately.
    (b) bring their families together and discuss the matter.
    (c) clean the car a little bit better the next time.
    (d) arrive earlier for the bus.

    Indicate your answer by putting **a, b, c** or **d** in the box provided. ☐

Fourth Part

You will now hear **four** news items taken from the radio, followed by the weather forecast. The news will be played **three** times; the first time right through, then in five segments with pauses, and finally right through again.

(Item 1)   `CD1 Track 35`

1. (i)   Who was driving the car?

_____

(ii)   What caused the accident? Give **two** reasons.

_____

_____

(Item 2)   `CD1 Track 36`

2. (i)   Where is the traffic chaos at its worst?

_____

(ii)   What gave rise to such chaos on the roads? Give **two** details.

_____

_____

(Item 3)   `CD1 Track 37`

3. (i)   Where did the accident happen?

_____

(ii)   What happened as a result of the accident? Give **one** detail.

_____

(Item 4)   `CD1 Track 38`

4. (i)   When did the accident happen?

_____

(ii)   What age was the driver who caused the accident?

_____

(Item 5)   `CD1 Track 39`

5. Weather Forecast
(i)   What type of weather is forecast for Sunday morning? Give **two** details.

_____

_____

(ii)   Give **two** details of the weather expected for Sunday afternoon.

_____

Revision 2

CD4

1. List the **ten** years mentioned on the CD.

_____   _____

_____   _____

_____   _____

_____   _____

_____   _____

2. Parts of the body.
   Translate the **ten** parts of the body mentioned on the CD.

_____   _____

_____   _____

_____   _____

_____   _____

_____   _____

3. Weather.
   Translate the **ten** weather topics mentioned on the CD.

_____   _____

_____   _____

_____   _____

_____   _____

_____   _____

4. Geography.
   Translate the **ten** geographical items mentioned on the CD.

_____   _____

_____   _____

_____   _____

_____   _____

_____   _____

5. Health.
   Translate the **ten** sicknesses mentioned on the CD.

_____   _____

_____   _____

_____   _____

_____   _____

Wortschatz

der Rollstuhl – *wheelchair*
die Blindheit – *blindness*
körperbehindert – *having a physical disability*
geistig behindert – *having a mental disability*
ausgeschlossen – *excluded*
die Punktschrift (Braille-Schrift) – *Braille*
breite Türeingänge – *wide doorways*
die Diskriminierung – *discrimination*
(querschnitt)gelähmt – *paralysed*
Minderwertigkeitskomplex – *inferiority complex*

Test 5

German – Ordinary Level
LISTENING COMPREHENSION

First Part

CD1 Track 42

The interview will be played **three** times – the second time with pauses.

1. (i)   Where does Herr Treige live?

    _____

    (ii) How long has he been in a wheelchair?

    _____

2. (i)   Herr Treige was involved in an accident. Mention any **two** details?

    _____

    _____

    (ii) How long did he spend in hospital?

    _____

3. What did Herr Treige do after coming out of hospital?

    _____

    _____

4. (i) What does Herr Treige's work consist of?

_____

_____

(ii) Mention **two** things he likes about his job.

_____

_____

5. (i) What difficulties does Herr Treige encounter in his daily life? Mention any **two**.

_____

_____

(ii) What activities does he miss most? Mention any **two**.

_____

_____

Second Part

CD1 Track 43

You will now hear a telephone conversation **three** times. The receptionist takes a message from the caller.

1. What is the caller ringing about? Give **two** details.

_____

_____

2. The receptionist is friendly. Give **two** details to show this.

_____

_____

3. What are the name and the phone number of the caller?

Name: _____

Phone Number: _____

4. The phonecall is to:
(a) a youth centre
(b) a youth hostel
(c) a hospital
(d) a day care centre

Indicate your answer by putting **a**, **b**, **c** or **d** in the box provided. ☐

CD1 Track 44

Third Part

You will now hear a conversation between two people. The dialogue will be played **three** times, with a pause after each playing. Answer in English.

1. (i)   How long has Julia been out of school?

    _____

    (ii) Why was she out of school for so long? Give **two** details.

    _____

    _____

2. (i)   Mention **one** way that Christian will help her to fit back into the class.

    _____

    (ii) Who else will help her?

    _____

3. Mention any **two** worries that Julia has about school work.

    _____

    _____

4. At the end of the conversation, Christian decides to:
    (a) arrange a class outing.
    (b) go on a school tour.
    (c) have a party at his house for the class.
    (d) help Julia after school.

    Indicate your answer by putting **a, b, c** or **d** in the box provided.   ☐

Fourth Part

You will now hear **four** news items taken from the radio, followed by the weather forecast. The news will be played **three** times; the first time right through, then in five segments with pauses, and finally right through again.

(Item 1)

CD1 Track 45

1. (i)   The Foundation for Reading has released some surprising findings. What are these?

    _____

    _____

    (ii) Where, according to the Foundation spokesperson, does the blame lie? Mention **two** points the spokesperson makes to support the claim.

    _____

    _____

(Item 2)   `CD1 Track 46`

2. (i)   Describe the new initiative in Wickede, mentioning **two** details.

_____

_____

(ii)   How much money do the families receive in payment?

_____

(Item 3)   `CD1 Track 47`

3. (i)   Give **two** details of those involved in the scheme for disabled children in Hagen.

_____

_____

(ii)   What services will the centre provide? Mention **two** details.

_____

_____

(Item 4)   `CD1 Track 48`

4. (i)   How long has *Aktion Sorgenkind* been in existence?

_____

(ii)   Mention **two** kinds of institutions which are supported financially by the charity.

_____

_____

(Item 5)   `CD1 Track 49`

5. Weather Forecast
    What type of weather is expected:
    (i)   for today? Give **two** details.

_____

_____

(ii)   for tomorrow? Give **two** details.

_____

_____

Computer

Einheit 6

Wortschatz

der Computer(-) – *computer*
der PC – *PC/computer*
der Laptop(-s) – *laptop*
die Maus – *mouse*
das Computerspiel(-e) – *computer game*
der Chatraum(-räume) – *chat room*
die Webseite(-n) – *web page*
der Nutzer(-) – *user(s)*
emailen – *to email*
die Email – *email*
das Internet – *internet*
ins Internet gehen – *to go on the internet*
meine eigene Facebook-Seite – *my own Facebook page*
die Datei(-en) – *file*
speichern – *to save*
das Laufwerk – *driver*
die Festplatte – *hard drive*
laden – *to load*
der Drucker – *printer*

Test 6

German – Ordinary Level

LISTENING COMPREHENSION

First Part

CD1 Track 52

The interview will be played **three** times – the second time with pauses.

1. (i)   How long has Frau Spengler been working in the post-office?

_____

    (ii) On what date did she begin working there?

_____

2. (i) What did a typical working day consist of in the past? Give **two** details.

_____

_____

 (ii) How has Eva's work changed? Mention **two** details.

_____

_____

3. (i) Mention **three** items that have been introduced recently for sale in the post-office.

_____

_____

_____

 (ii) Why is business so good? Give **one** reason.

_____

4. Mention **two** reasons why people no longer use traditional postal services as much as they used to.

_____

_____

5. Describe Eva's training. Mention any **two** details.

_____

_____

Second Part

CD1 Track 53

You will now hear a telephone conversation **three** times. The receptionist takes a message from the caller.

1. Why is the caller making this phonecall? Give details.

_____

_____

2. How does the caller explain that the items cannot be his?

_____

_____

3. What are the name and the phone number of the caller?

   Name: _____

   Phone Number: _____

4. The phonecall is to:
   (a) a local supermarket.
   (b) a furniture store.
   (c) a computer firm.
   (d) a fitness centre.

   Indicate your answer by putting **a, b, c** or **d** in the box provided. ☐

Third Part

CD1 Track 54

Peter Kux speaks about his present job and how he came to be in it. The dialogue will be played **three** times, with a pause after each playing. Answer in English.

1. Where is the hospital in which Peter works situated? Give **two** details.

   _____

   _____

2. (i) What are the most common sport and traffic injuries for which patients in this hospital are treated?

   _____

   _____

   (ii) What do many of the elderly patients suffer from? Give **two** details.

   _____

   _____

3. Describe the work Peter does in the hospital.

   _____

   _____

4. Peter's life has had its disappointments. Outline any **one** instance from his past that shows this.

   _____

5. Explain why Peter does not like his present job.

   _____

   _____

Fourth Part

You will now hear **four** news items taken from the radio, followed by the weather forecast. The news will be played **three** times; the first time right through, then in five segments with pauses, and finally right through again.

(Item 1)   `CD1 Track 55`

1. (i)   What is the theme of the project week Netdays?

_____

(ii)   What is the latest date for entering?

_____

(Item 2)   `CD1 Track 56`

2. (i)   What warning has been issued by computer experts?

_____

_____

(ii)   When was it discovered?

_____

(Item 3)   `CD1 Track 57`

3. (i)   What percentage of German internet users chooses not to shop online?

_____

(ii)   Mention any **two** reasons why this is the case.

_____

_____

(Item 4)   `CD1 Track 58`

4. (i)   Germans spend more and more money booking travel tickets online.
How much money did they spend last year?

_____

(ii)   Who profits mainly from this new trend? Give **one** example.

_____

(Item 5)   `CD1 Track 59`

5. Weather Forecast
(i)   What will weather conditions be like today?

_____

(ii)   What is the forecast for tomorrow?

_____

Revision 3

CD4

1. List the **ten** dates mentioned on the CD.

_____   _____

_____   _____

_____   _____

_____   _____

_____   _____

2. Cars.
   Translate the **ten** car-related items mentioned on the CD.

_____   _____

_____   _____

_____   _____

_____   _____

_____   _____

3. Federal states.
   List the **ten** federal states (*Bundesländer*) mentioned on the CD.

_____   _____

_____   _____

_____   _____

_____   _____

_____   _____

4. List the **five** names spelled out on the CD.

_____

_____

_____

_____

_____

5. Materials.
   Translate the **ten** materials mentioned on the CD.

_____   _____

_____   _____

_____   _____

_____   _____

Wortschatz

die Ausbeutung – *exploitation*
die Hilfsorganisation(-en) – *aid organisation*
karitative Organisation(-en) – *charitable organisation*
der Völkermord – *genocide*
spenden – *to donate*
die Spende(-n) – *donation*
die Hungersnot(-nöte) – *famine*
die Dürre(-n) – *drought*
die Kinderarbeit – *child labour*
die Sklaverei – *slavery*
der Sklave(-n) – *slave(s)*
verhungern – *to starve to death*
verdursten – *to die of thirst*
die Krankheit(-en) – *illness*
sauberes Wasser – *clean water*
der Hungerlohn – *starvation wage*
das Straßenkind(-er) – *street child*
die Überbevölkerung – *over-population*

Test 7

German – Ordinary Level

LISTENING COMPREHENSION

First Part

CD1 Track 62

The interview will be played **three** times – the second time with pauses.

1. (i) For how long has the Vocational School in Altötting been involved in Third World projects?

_____

   (ii) The use of solar energy for cooking has become very necessary in some parts of Africa. Mention **one** of the reasons given.

_____

2. (i) How many solar cookers are provided per village?

   _____

   (ii) List **two** advantages of the solar cooker.

   _____

   _____

3. Whose idea was it to produce solar cookers?

   _____

4. How many solar cookers have been made so far in Uganda?

   _____

5. Johannes held a workshop in Uganda. Give **two** details.

   _____

   _____

Second Part

CD1 Track 63

You will now hear a telephone conversation **three** times. The receptionist takes a message from the caller.

1. Why is the caller making this phonecall? Give details.

   _____

   _____

2. The caller is enthusiastic. Give **two** details to show this.

   _____

   _____

3. What are the name and the phone number of the caller?

   Name: _____

   Phone Number: _____

4. The caller wants to:
   (a) study for a year first.
   (b) spend a year abroad before commencing her studies.
   (c) do a First Aid course.
   (d) work in an office.

   Indicate your answer by putting **a**, **b**, **c** or **d** in the box provided. ☐

Third Part

You will now hear a conversation between Frau Hoppe and Christian. The dialogue will be played **three** times, with a pause after each playing. Answer in English.

1. Frau Hoppe meets Christian after he returns home from abroad. Where has he been and how long did he spend there?

   Where: _____

   How long: _____

2. What preparation did Christian make before doing his year abroad?

   _____

   _____

3. Give **three** details of the work he was involved in abroad.

   _____

   _____

   _____

4. Christian now knows what he wants to do in the future:
   (a) He wants to improve his English.
   (b) He wants to study in India.
   (c) He wants to work abroad again.
   (d) He wants to be a doctor.

   Indicate your answer by putting **a**, **b**, **c** or **d** in the box provided. ☐

Fourth Part

You will now hear **four** news items taken from the radio, followed by the weather forecast. The news will be played **three** times; the first time right through, then in five segments with pauses, and finally right through again.

(Item 1)

1. (i) How much money will be spent on fireworks on New Year's Eve? Give details.

   _____

   _____

   (ii) How much money did *Brot für die Welt* collect over the entire year?

   _____

   _____

(Item 2)   CD1 Track 66

2. (i)   How many were killed and injured in the accident?

_____

_____

   (ii) In what country did the accident take place?

_____

(Item 3)   CD1 Track 67

3. What rights in particular does the spokesman want to achieve for children?

_____

_____

(Item 4)   CD1 Track 68

4. (i)   How many people were killed in the typhoon?

_____

   (ii) How many typhoons have struck the Philippines this year?

_____

_____

(Item 5)   CD1 Track 69

5. Weather Forecast
    (i)   Where is snow expected to fall?

_____

_____

   (ii) What temperatures are expected for today and tonight?

_____

_____

Wortschatz

der Alkohol – *alcohol*
der Alkoholkonsum – *the consumption of alcohol*
die Droge(-n) – *drug(s)*
drogenabhängig – *addicted to drugs*
das Rauschgift – *drugs*
der Drogenhändler(-) – *drug dealer(s)*
die Tablette(-n) – *tablet(s)*
die Sucht – *addiction*
der/die Süchtige – *addict*
der Gruppenzwang – *peer pressure*
süchtig – *addicted*
schmuggeln – *to smuggle*
inhalieren – *to inhale*
rauchen – *to smoke*
spritzen – *to inject*
Gesundheitsschäden – *damage to health*
das Selbstwertgefühl – *self-esteem*
die Kriminalität – *crime*
sterben – *to die*

Test 8

German – Ordinary Level

LISTENING COMPREHENSION

First Part

CD2 Track 2

Listen to the CD. The interview will be played **three** times – the second time with pauses.

1. What do you learn about Frau Steinhoff? Give **two** details.

   _____

   _____

2. (i)   What age was Frau Steinhoff's daughter when she started taking drugs?

    _____

    (ii) What reasons does she give for not noticing?

    _____

    _____

3. What changes did Frau Steinhoff's sister notice in the daughter's behaviour?
    Mention any **two**.

    _____

    _____

4. (i)   What evidence finally convinced her of her daughter's use of drugs?

    _____

    _____

    (ii) Mention **one** other indicator that something was not right.

    _____

5. (i)   Does her daughter still take drugs? Give **two** details.

    _____

    _____

    (ii) What plans does her daughter have for the future? Give **two** details.

    _____

    _____

Second Part

CD2 Track 3

You will now hear a telephone conversation **three** times. The receptionist takes a message from the caller.

1. Why is the caller making this phonecall? Give details.

    _____

    _____

2. What made the caller suspicious? Give **one** detail.

    _____

3. What are the name and the phone number of the caller?

    Name: _____

    Phone Number: _____

4. The caller will:
    (a) receive a visit shortly.
    (b) come to meet the man she rang.
    (c) go to a hospital.
    (d) have no more to do with the matter.

    Indicate your answer by putting **a**, **b**, **c** or **d** in the box provided. ☐

Third Part

You will now hear a conversation between **two** people. The dialogue will be played **three** times, with a pause after each playing. Answer in English.

1. What age is Petra and what kind of school does she attend?

    Age: _____

    School: _____

2. When does Petra normally drink alcohol?

    _____

    _____

3. How often does Petra drink alcohol?

    _____

    _____

4. What do her parents think of this?

    _____

    _____

Fourth Part

You will now hear **four** news items taken from the radio, followed by the weather forecast. The news will be played **three** times; the first time right through, then in five segments with pauses, and finally right through again.

(Item 1) [CD2 Track 5]
1. Where in Germany can cannabis now be legally obtained for medical use?

    _____

    _____

    _____

(Item 2)   CD2 Track 6

2. (i)   More and more young Germans smoke. What age group is most affected?

_____

_____

    (ii) Do more boys or girls smoke? What are the exact percentages for each group?

_____

_____

(Item 3)   CD2 Track 7

3. (i)   What are the main findings of the study mentioned here? Give **two** details.

_____

_____

    (ii) Give **two** details of those involved in the study.

_____

_____

(Item 4)   CD2 Track 8

4. (i)   What did customs officials discover?

_____

_____

    (ii) Where was the discovery made?

_____

_____

(Item 5)   CD2 Track 9

5. Weather Forecast
    What type of weather is expected:
    (i)   for today? Give **two** details.

_____

_____

    (ii) for the coming week? Give **two** details.

_____

_____

Revision 4

1. Prices.
    List the **ten** prices mentioned on the CD.

    _____   _____
    _____   _____
    _____   _____
    _____   _____
    _____   _____

2. Catastrophes.
    Translate the **ten** catastrophes mentioned on the CD.

    _____   _____
    _____   _____
    _____   _____
    _____   _____
    _____   _____

3. Car accidents.
    Translate the words and sentences related to accidents that are mentioned on the CD.

    _____   _____
    _____   _____
    _____   _____
    _____   _____
    _____   _____

4. Environment.
    Translate the **ten** environmental topics mentioned on the CD.

    _____   _____
    _____   _____
    _____   _____
    _____   _____
    _____   _____

5. In the home.
    Translate the **ten** household items mentioned on the CD.

    _____   _____
    _____   _____
    _____   _____
    _____   _____
    _____   _____

Wortschatz

sich vertragen mit (+ Dat.) – *to get on with*
auskommen mit (+Dat.) – *to get on with*
schimpfen mit – *to give out to*
die Hausarbeit – *housework*
behandeln – *to treat*
drohen(+ Dat.) – *to threaten*
verprügeln – *to beat*
die Kindesmisshandlung – *child abuse*
die Verwahrlosung – *neglect*
das Taschengeld – *pocket-money*
streng – *strict*
lässig – *easy-going*
der Streit – *quarrel*
ünterstützen – *to support*
die Unterstützung – *support*
der Lärm – *noise*
sich zanken – *to quarrel*

Test 9

German – Ordinary Level

LISTENING COMPREHENSION

First Part   CD2 Track 12

Listen to the CD. The interview will be played **three** times – the second time with pauses.

1. (i)   Which section of the newspaper does Heike want to look at?

    _____

    (ii) What objections does her father offer? Mention any **two**.

    _____

    _____

2. What does Heike's morning look like at present? Mention **two** details.

_____

_____

3. What arguments does she use to persuade her father? Mention any **three**.

_____

_____

_____

4. (i) What details are we given about Silvia? Mention any **two**.

_____

_____

(ii) Why might Heike be able to share with Silvia?

_____

5. (i) Why is Heike's father now in favour of her proposal?

_____

_____

(ii) How does he propose helping Heike with her decision? Mention **one** detail.

_____

Second Part

CD2 Track 13

You will now hear a telephone conversation **three** times. The secretary of Action Concept in Cologne takes a message.

1. What does the caller first want to check with Action Concept about his daughter?

_____

_____

2. What kind of activities does the caller imagine his daughter taking part in? Give **two** details.

_____

_____

3. What are the name and the phone number of the caller?

Name: _____

Phone Number: _____

4. The phonecall is to:
   (a) a leisure centre.
   (b) a stunt school.
   (c) a drug rehabilitation unit.
   (d) a film studio.

   Indicate your answer by putting **a**, **b**, **c** or **d** in the box provided. ☐

Third Part
CD2 Track 14

You will now hear a conversation between two people. The dialogue will be played **three** times, with a pause after each playing. Answer in English.

1. At the start of the conversation, what does the son offer to do for his mother?

   _____

   _____

   _____

2. What **two** items of post have arrived?

   _____

   _____

3. Why does the mother get such a shock upon opening the second envelope? Give details.

   _____

   _____

   _____

4. What explanation does the son give his mother?
   (a) He rang his friend in Turkey.
   (b) He posted items to Turkey.
   (c) He ordered items from Turkey.
   (d) He bought a plane ticket to Turkey.

   Indicate your answer by putting **a**, **b**, **c** or **d** in the box provided. ☐

Fourth Part

You will now hear **four** news items taken from the radio, followed by the weather forecast. The news will be played **three** times; the first time right through, then in five segments with pauses, and finally right through again.

(Item 1)   `CD2 Track 15`

1. (i)   Why was the couple brought before the court?

    _____

    _____

    (ii) What had their son done?

    _____

    _____

(Item 2)   `CD2 Track 16`

2. What service does *Schüler Notruf Center* provide? Mention any **two** details.

    _____

    _____

(Item 3)   `CD2 Track 17`

3. (i)   What percentage of children suffer from poverty?

    _____

    (ii) When was the study published?

    _____

(Item 4)   `CD2 Track 18`

4. (i)   What proposal was made by the CSU General Secretary?

    _____

    _____

    (ii) What types of crime are typical for young culprits, according to the
          General Secretary? Mention any **one**.

    _____

    _____

(Item 5)   `CD2 Track 19`

5. Weather Forecast
    (i)   What is the weather forecast for today? Mention three details?

    _____

    _____

    (ii) What is the weather forecast for the next day?

    _____

    _____

    _____

Jobben

Einheit 10

Wortschatz

arbeiten – *to work*
der Verdienst – *earnings*
verdienen – *to earn*
Guthaben – *credit*
das Handy(-s) – *mobile phone*
ausgehen – *to go out*
sich (Dat.) leisten – *to afford*
Regale auffüllen – *to stack shelves*
babysitten – *to babysit*
die Kasse – *till*
als Kellner/-in – *as a waiter/waitress*

Test 10

German – Ordinary Level

LISTENING COMPREHENSION

First Part

CD2 Track 22

Listen to the CD. The interview will be played **three** times – the second time with pauses.

1. Why is Anna fed up? Explain giving **two** details.

   _____

   _____

2. Thomas has found work.
   (i) How did he get the job?

   _____

   (ii) What does the job entail? Mention **one** detail.

   _____

3. What details does Thomas give about pay and work times? Mention **three** details.

_____

_____

_____

4. How long does a tour last and how many people are in a group?

_____

_____

5. Anna is interested in Thomas's work.
   (i) What are the requirements for getting this kind of job? Mention any **two**.

   _____

   _____

   (ii) Apart from money, what are the other benefits of this kind of work? Mention any **two**.

   _____

   _____

Second Part
CD2 Track 23

You will now hear a telephone conversation **three** times. The receptionist takes a message from the caller.

1. What problem is the caller concerned about and why? Give **two** details.

   _____

   _____

2. What are the name and the phone number of the caller?

   Name: _____

   Phone Number: _____

3. What is the name of the person who is going to ring the caller back?

   _____

4. The phonecall is to the office of:
   (a) a theatre festival.
   (b) a gardening show.
   (c) a job centre.
   (d) a leisure park.

   Indicate your answer by putting **a, b, c** or **d** in the box provided.

Third Part

CD2 Track 24

You will now hear a conversation between two people. The dialogue will be played **three** times, with a pause after each playing. Answer in English.

1. (i)   Why is Herr Kramer so annoyed?

    _____

    _____

    (ii) Where is Frau Lorenz doing her work experience?

    _____

    _____

2. Why is Frau Lorenz so uninterested in her work?

    _____

    _____

3. Mention **two** aspects of her work experience that particularly annoy Frau Lorenz.

    _____

    _____

4. Herr Kramer suggests making the best of things because:
    (a) Frau Lorenz has three more years to go.
    (b) she has already served half her time.
    (c) she has to put in two more weeks.
    (d) she will get used to the work.

    Indicate your answer by putting **a**, **b**, **c** or **d** in the box provided.

Fourth Part

You will now hear **four** news items taken from the radio, followed by the weather forecast. The news will be played **three** times; the first time right through, then in five segments with pauses, and finally right through again.

(Item 1)

CD2 Track 25

1. Mention any **two** details of the Youth Protection Act (*Jugendschutzgesetz*).

    _____

    _____

(Item 2)   CD2 Track 26

2. (i) What is the minimum age for young people who wish to work part-time?

_____

(ii) Between which times are young people allowed to work? Mention **one** exception to these limits.

_____

_____

(Item 3)   CD2 Track 27

3. (i) According to the study, what percentage of students work during term-time?

_____

(ii) What proportion work during holiday-time?

_____

(Item 4)   CD2 Track 28

4. (i) What are school students in Hamburg planning to do on 'Day for Africa'?

_____

_____

(ii) How many pupils are participating?

_____

(Item 5)   CD2 Track 29

5. Weather Forecast
What kind of weather is expected for:
(i) today?

_____

_____

(ii) tomorrow?

_____

_____

Revision 5

1. List the **ten** numbers mentioned on the CD.

_____   _____
_____   _____
_____   _____
_____   _____
_____   _____

2. Home.
   Translate the **ten** household words mentioned on the CD.

_____   _____
_____   _____
_____   _____
_____   _____
_____   _____

3. Travel.
   Translate the **ten** travel items mentioned on the CD.

_____   _____
_____   _____
_____   _____
_____   _____
_____   _____

4. Reading Materials.
   Translate the **ten** reading materials mentioned on the CD.

_____   _____
_____   _____
_____   _____
_____   _____
_____   _____

5. Clothing.
   Translate the **ten** items of clothing mentioned on the CD.

_____   _____
_____   _____
_____   _____
_____   _____

Wortschatz

mobben – *to bully*
Mobbing – *bullying*
einschüchtern – *to intimidate*
das Opfer(-) – *victim*
der/die Täter/in – *culprit*
die Gewalt – *violence*
ausgrenzen – *to isolate/exclude*
schlagen – *to hit*
anpöbeln – *to abuse (slang)*
beschimpfen – *to insult*
zusammenschlagen – *to beat up*
die Angst – *fear*
strafen – *to punish*
Streber(-) – *swot*
der Schleimer(-) – *bootlicker/toady (slang)*
Geld erpressen – *to extort money*
leistungsstark – *good (performing)*
leistungsschwach – *weak (performing)*

Test 11

German – Ordinary Level

LISTENING COMPREHENSION

First Part

CD2 Track 32

Listen to the CD. The interview will be played **three** times – the second time with pauses.

1. What do we learn about Jan L. from the interviewer? Mention **two** details.

   _____

   _____

2. (i)   According to Dr Richter, what statistics show that bullying is a widespread problem?

    _____

    _____

    (ii) What advice does he give to those who feel threatened? Give **one** detail.

    _____

3. (i)   How should one react if one sees someone being beaten up in school?

    _____

    _____

    (ii) What should one do if one notices a fight about to begin?

    _____

    _____

4. What should one say to those acting in an aggressive manner or consuming alcohol and other drugs? Mention **two** details.

    _____

    _____

5. (i)   In what ways does bullying by girls differ from that by boys?

    _____

    _____

    (ii) What concrete advice does Dr Richter give Jan L.'s parents?

    _____

    _____

Second Part

CD2 Track 33

You will now hear a telephone conversation **three** times. Frau Meier takes a message from the caller.

1. Who is the message for?

    _____

2. What problem is the caller concerned about?

    _____

    _____

3. What are the name and the telephone number of the caller?

    Name: _____

    Phone Number: _____

4. After listening to the phonecall for the **third** time, tick the correct answer.

    The phonecall is to:
    (a) a library.
    (b) a police station.
    (c) a hospital.
    (d) a school.

    Indicate your answer by putting **a**, **b**, **c** or **d** in the box provided. ☐

Third Part

CD2 Track 34

You will now hear a conversation between Angela and Ulf. The dialogue will be played **three** times, with a pause after each playing. Answer in English.

1. (i) What do Angela and Ulf talk about at the start of the conversation?

    _____

    (ii) All of a sudden, Ulf's attention is drawn to something else. What distracts him?

    _____

    _____

2. What does Angela find out? Give details.

    _____

    _____

3. What practical help does Angela offer Ulf?

    _____

    _____

4. Which of the following steps will Ulf now take?

    (a) Talk to the school counsellor.
    (b) Talk to the police.
    (c) Talk to somebody on a help line.
    (d) Talk to their class teacher.

    Indicate your answer by putting **a**, **b**, **c** or **d** in the box provided. ☐

Fourth Part

You will now hear **four** news items taken from the radio, followed by the weather forecast. The news will be played **three** times; the first time right through, then in five segments with pauses, and finally right through again.

(Item 1)   CD2 Track 35

1. (i) What prison term was handed down to the girl?

_____

(ii) What other punishment did she receive?

_____

_____

(Item 2)   CD2 Track 36

2. (i) Give **two** details of the study carried out by the University of Lindau.

_____

_____

(ii) How many pupils in Germany have been the victims of cyber-bullying?

_____

(Item 3)   CD2 Track 37

3. (i) What statistics does the EU quote to back up its claims about cyber-bullying?

_____

_____

(ii) Give **one** detail about 'Safe Internet Day'.

_____

(Item 4)   CD2 Track 38

4. Who started the anti-bullying initiative and what does he hope to achieve?

_____

_____

(Item 5)   CD2 Track 39

5. Weather Forecast
(i) To which states does the weather forecast apply?

_____

_____

(ii) What type of weather is forecast for today? Give **two** details.

_____

_____

Wortschatz

kennen lernen – *to get to know*
besprechen – *to discuss*
diskutieren – *to discuss (general)*
die Eigenschaft(-en) – *quality*
der Freund(-e) – *male friend/boyfriend*
die Freundin(-innen) – *female friend/girlfriend*
lieben – *to love*
die Liebe – *love*
sich verlieben – *to fall in love*
Schluss machen mit (+Dat.) – *to break it off with*
miteinander gehen – *to go with one another*
sich treffen mit (+ Dat.) – *to meet (by arrangement)*
ablenken – *to distract*
erzählen – *to tell*

Test 12

German – Ordinary Level
LISTENING COMPREHENSION

First Part

CD2 Track 42

Listen to the CD. The interview will be played **three** times – the second time with pauses.

1. (i) Hannes works in a Children's Hospital. What is his job title in English?

    (ii) Why does Hannes consider laughter to be the best medicine for sick children?

2. (i) How long did Hannes' training take?

(ii) What are the name (in English) and location of the training school he attended?

Name: _____

Location: _____

3. Give **three** details regarding what Hannes learned during his training.

_____

_____

_____

4. How does Hannes prepare for his job in the morning? Give **three** details.

_____

_____

_____

5. (i) Hannes visited a little girl that morning. What was her age and nationality?

_____

_____

(ii) What trick did he perform while he was with her?

_____

_____

Second Part

CD2 Track 43

You will now hear a telephone conversation **three** times. Peter has to pass on a message from the caller to a friend of his.

1. Why is Angela so happy? Give **two** details.

_____

_____

2. Peter will see Mark again before Angela does. When and where will Peter meet Mark?

When: _____

Where: _____

3. What does Angela wish Peter to say to Mark when he meets him?

_____

_____

4. (i) Where will Angela be if Mark wants to phone her?

_____

_____

(ii) What is the telephone number there?

_____

Third Part   `CD2 Track 44`

You will now hear a conversation between two people. The dialogue will be played **three** times, with a pause after each playing. Answer in English.

1. Marie has suddenly heard the news that she did not expect about Dirk's plans. She speaks to Dirk about it.

   (i) How did she hear about Dirk's plans?

   _____

   _____

   (ii) What is Dirk seemingly planning to do?

   _____

   _____

   _____

2. Marie is upset. Why did the news upset her so much?

   _____

   _____

   _____

3. Give **two** reasons (from the conversation) why young people would want to leave the island of Helgoland.

   _____

   _____

4. Dirk wants to go to Hamburg:

   (a) as soon as he has earned enough money to pay for a flat there.
   (b) with Marie in a few years time.
   (c) to be with a friend who is there already.
   (d) to get proper dental treatment there.

   Indicate your answer by putting **a, b, c** or **d** in the box provided. ☐

Fourth Part

You will now hear **four** news items taken from the radio, followed by the weather forecast. The news will be played **three** times; the first time right through, then in five segments with pauses, and finally right through again.

(Item 1)   CD2 Track 45

1. (i) What special offer is available from the marketing company?

_____

   (ii) What is Facebook against?

_____

(Item 2)   CD2 Track 46

2. (i) From which countries do the young people come? Mention any **three**.

_____

_____

_____

   (ii) What are the young people asked to do? Give **two** details.

_____

_____

(Item 3)   CD2 Track 47

3. (i) What is the main finding issued by the scientists?

_____

_____

   (ii) In which cases are friendships particularly important? Mention any **two**.

_____

_____

(Item 4)   CD2 Track 48

4. (i) Which **two** countries are mentioned here?

_____

_____

   (ii) What is the significance of the Oder-Neisse Line?

_____

_____

(Item 5)   CD2 Track 49

5. Weather Forecast

(i)   What has caused the change in the weather? Give **two** details.

_____

_____

(ii) What type of weather is forecast for today? Give **two** details.

_____

_____

Revision 6

CD4

1. Weights and measures.
   List the **five** measures and **five** weights mentioned on the CD.

   _____   _____

   _____   _____

   _____   _____

   _____   _____

   _____   _____

2. Part-time jobs.
   Translate the **ten** part-time jobs mentioned on the CD.

   _____   _____

   _____   _____

   _____   _____

   _____   _____

   _____   _____

3. Work.
   Translate the **ten** work-related vocabulary items mentioned on the CD.

   _____   _____

   _____   _____

   _____   _____

   _____   _____

   _____   _____

4. Industries.
   Translate the **ten** industries mentioned on the CD.

   _____   _____

   _____   _____

   _____   _____

   _____   _____

   _____   _____

5. Means of transport.
   Translate the **ten** means of transport mentioned on the CD.

   _____   _____

   _____   _____

   _____   _____

   _____   _____

Wortschatz

der Deutsche/die Deutsche – *German man/woman*
die Deutschen – *the Germans*
Menschen deutscher Abstammung – *people of German origin*
lässig – *casual/easy-going*
das Bundesland (-länder) – *federal state*
der Bundeskanzler/die Bundeskanzlerin – *Federal Chancellor (= Taoiseach)*
der Bundestag – *parliament (= Dáil)*
der/die Bundestagsabgeordnete – *Member of Parliament (= TD)*
die Insel(n) – *island(s)*
die Bevölkerung – *population*
das Essen – *food*
das Wetter – *weather*
das Klima – *climate*
die Kriminalität – *crime*
sportlich – *into sport*
musikalisch – *musical*
der Sinn für Humor – *sense of humour*
das Klischee(-s) – *cliché*
die Konjunktur – *economy/economic activity*
das Wirtschaftswunder – *economic miracle*
der Gastarbeiter(-) – *guest workers (immigrant workers)*
die Berliner Mauer – *the Berlin wall*
die Teilung deutschlands – *partition of Germany*
die Wiedervereinigung – *reunification*
der Erste/der Zweite Weltkrieg – *the First/Second World War*
das Dritte Reich – *the Third Reich*

Test 13

German – Ordinary Level

LISTENING COMPREHENSION

First Part

CD2 Track 52

Listen to the CD. The interview will be played **three** times – the second time with pauses.

1. (i) What does Herr Saris work at?

   _____

   (ii) How many foreigners work there altogether?

   _____

2. (i) How many hours does he work per week?

   _____

   (ii) How much holidays does he get? Where and when does he spend them?

   _____

   _____

3. In earlier years, Herr Saris helped out in the personnel section.
   (i) On what day of the week did he work there?

   _____

   (ii) Mention **two** problems he dealt with.

   _____

   _____

4. Mention **two** things he says about the Germans.

   _____

   _____

5. Mention **one** positive aspect and **one** negative aspect that Herr Saris finds about living in Germany.

   _____

   _____

Second Part

CD2 Track 53

You will now hear a telephone conversation **three** times. The receptionist takes a message from the caller.

1. Who does the caller wish to speak to?

   _____

2. What problem is the caller concerned about? Give **two** details.

   _____

   _____

3. What are the name and the phone number of the caller?

Name: _____

Telephone Number: _____

4. The phonecall is to:
   (a) a youth club.
   (b) a youth hostel.
   (c) a hotel.
   (d) a cinema.

Indicate your answer by putting **a**, **b**, **c** or **d** in the box provided. ☐

Third Part

CD2 Track 54

You will now hear a conversation between two people. The dialogue will be played **three** times, with a pause after each playing.

1. (i) Why is Regina so annoyed with Werner at the start of the conversation? Give **one** reason.

_____

   (ii) What excuse does Werner give for not contacting her?

_____

2. (i) What bad news does Werner tell Regina about his job?

_____

   (ii) How does Regina respond to this? Give **two** details.

_____

_____

3. Werner suggests ways in which he and Regina could overcome any difficulties. Give **two** of these suggestions.

_____

_____

4. Werner has some surprising news for Regina towards the end of the conversation. He has:

   (a) won some money.
   (b) been promoted and will earn more money.
   (c) been asked to work abroad.
   (d) taken over the company.

Indicate your answer by putting **a**, **b**, **c** or **d** in the box provided. ☐

Fourth Part

You will now hear **four** news items taken from the radio, followed by the weather forecast. The news will be played **three** times; the first time right through, then in five segments with pauses, and finally right through again.

(Item 1)   `CD2 Track 55`

1. (i) **In what year** is this great world fair to take place, and **where**?

_____

_____

   (ii) How many visitors are expected to come there each day?

_____

(Item 2)   `CD2 Track 56`

2. Women in public service jobs.
   (i) To which month do the figures apply?

_____

   (ii) According to the statistics how many women were employed in the public service?

_____

(Item 3)   `CD2 Track 57`

3. (i) The Egmont publishing company carried out a recent study in Germany. Mention **two** details about the study.

_____

_____

   (ii) Mention **two** priority items on the shopping list of the people who were surveyed.

_____

_____

(Item 4)   `CD2 Track 58`

4. (i) How many people in Germany are estimated to be infected with AIDS?

_____

   (ii) Mention one service being provided by the Neuss Health Board?

_____

(Item 5)   `CD2 Track 59`

5. Weather Forecast
   (i) What type of weather is forecast for Monday?

_____

   (ii) What is the outlook for the next few days?

_____

_____

Wortschatz

obdachlos – *homeless*
die Obdachlosigkeit – *homelessness*
der/die Obdachlose(-n) – *the homeless person(s)*
das Mitleid – *sympathy*
das Obdachlosenasyl – *homeless shelter*
der Penner – *tramp*
das Straßenkind(-er) – *street child*
der Ausreißer – *runaway*
ausreißen – *to run away (from home)*
der Türeingang – *doorway*
die Bank – *bench*
betteln – *to beg*
die Almosen – *alm*
Essen auf Rädern – *Meals on Wheels*
die karitative Organisation – *charitable organisation*
erfrieren – *to freeze to death*
der Alkoholiker(-) – *alcoholic*
der/die Süchtige – *addict*
sich kümmern um (+Akk.) – *to look after/care for*

Test 14

German – Ordinary Level
LISTENING COMPREHENSION

First Part

CD2 Track 62

Listen to the CD. The interview will be played **three** times – the second time with pauses.

1. (i) Where is the hostel situated?

   _____

   (ii) Who does the hostel cater for?

   _____

   _____

2. (i) What services does the hostel provide for those who come there?
   Mention any **two**.

   _____

   _____

   (ii) Mention any **one** condition that the visitors have to fulfil if they wish to
   stay longer?

   _____

3. (i) Describe the room, mentioning **two** details.

   _____

   _____

   (ii) Why do young people come to the hostel? Mention any **one** reason.

   _____

4. What information are we given about Florian? Mention any **two** details.

   _____

   _____

5. (i) How do the visitors to the hostel spend their evenings after their meal?
   Mention any **two** details.

   _____

   _____

   (ii) How many young people sleep rough each night in Germany?

   _____

Second Part

CD2 Track 63

You will now hear a telephone conversation **three** times. The volunteer takes a message
from the caller.

1. Why is the caller making the phonecall?

   _____

   _____

   _____

2. Mention **two** items about which she is particularly angry.

   _____

   _____

3. What are the name and the phone number of the caller?

Name: _____

Telephone Number: _____

4. The person who takes the call suggests that the caller:
(a) should mind her own business.
(b) go to the police.
(c) work there as a volunteer.
(d) donate some money.

Indicate your answer by putting **a**, **b**, **c** or **d** in the box provided. ☐

Third Part

CD2 Track 64

You will now hear a conversation between two people. The dialogue will be played **three** times, with a pause after each playing.

1. (i) What is the name in English of the organisation for which Bastian works?

_____

(ii) How does Bastian know Frau Keitmann?

_____

2. (i) Mention **one** detail about Bastian's brother Frank.

_____

(ii) Where is Frank now?

_____

3. What exactly does Bastian do at night?

_____

_____

4. At the end of the conversation Frau Keitmann:
(a) agrees to help Bastian.
(b) offers Bastian a job.
(c) invites him to talk about his work to people in her place of work.
(d) donates money to the organisation.

Indicate your answer by putting **a**, **b**, **c** or **d** in the box provided. ☐

Fourth Part

You will now hear **four** news items taken from the radio, followed by the weather forecast. The news will be played **three** times; the first time right through, then in five segments with pauses, and finally right through again.

(Item 1)   CD2 Track 65

1. (i)   What has the survey in Hamburg revealed? Give details.

_____

_____

   (ii) How many people in Hamburg state that they are living rough?

_____

_____

(Item 2)   CD2 Track 66

2. (i)   By how much have donations to Verein CaFee gone down?

_____

_____

   (ii) What effect has this had on their work? Give **one** detail.

_____

(Item 3)   CD2 Track 67

3. (i)   According to this news item, what are the consequences of the floods in West Africa? Mention any **two**.

_____

_____

   (ii) How many refugees are there in Senegal?

_____

(Item 4)   CD2 Track 68

4. (i)   For whom is Caritas demanding more special assistance?

_____

   (ii) Mention **one** area in particular where more facilities are needed.

_____

(Item 5)   CD2 Track 69

5. Weather Forecast
   (i)   Name **one** state of Germany to which the forecast applies?

_____

   (ii) What is the weather forecast for tomorrow? Give **two** details.

_____

_____

Revision 7

1. Percentages.
   List the **ten** percentages mentioned on the CD.

   _____   _____

   _____   _____

   _____   _____

   _____   _____

   _____   _____

2. Work.
   Translate the **ten** work-related vocabulary items mentioned on the CD.

   _____   _____

   _____   _____

   _____   _____

   _____   _____

   _____   _____

3. School.
   Translate the **ten** school-related words mentioned on the CD.

   _____   _____

   _____   _____

   _____   _____

   _____   _____

   _____   _____

4. Eating and drinking.
   Translate the **ten** food and drink items mentioned on the CD.

   _____   _____

   _____   _____

   _____   _____

   _____   _____

   _____   _____

5. Feelings and emotions.
   Translate the **ten** feelings and emotions mentioned on the CD.

   _____   _____

   _____   _____

   _____   _____

   _____   _____

Wortschatz

die Rücksicht – *consideration*
anpöbeln – *to abuse (slang)*
(un)höflich – *(im)polite*
Rücksicht nehmen auf (+ Akk.) – *to have consideration for*
Respekt zeigen – *to show respect*
die Respektlosigkeit – *disrespect*
der Wert(e) – *value(s)*
(un)freundlich – *friendly*
ignorieren – *to ignore*
die Ellenbogengesellschaft – *elbow society*
Manieren – *manners*
das Benehmen – *behaviour*
beleidigen – *to insult*
der Lärm – *noise*
diskriminieren – *to discriminate*
auslachen – *to make fun of/laugh at*
die Zivilcourage – *courage of one's convictions*
die (In-)Toleranz – *(in-)tolerance*

Test 15

German – Ordinary Level

LISTENING COMPREHENSION

First Part

CD3 Track 2

Listen to the CD. The interview will be played **three** times – the second time with pauses.

1. (i)   Where is Stefan working?

    _____

    _____

    (ii) How long has he been working there?

    _____

2. (i) Mention any **three** institutions in which this type of social service (*Zivildienst*) is possible?

_____

_____

_____

(ii) How long does the social service last?

_____

3. Describe what Stefan has to do as part of the morning shift.

_____

_____

_____

4. What does he particularly like about the work he is doing at present?

_____

_____

_____

5. What reasons does Stefan give for not wanting to do military service? Give details.

_____

_____

_____

Second Part

CD3 Track 3

You will now hear a telephone conversation **three** times. The receptionist takes a message from the caller.

1. Who is the message for?

_____

_____

2. What problem is the caller concerned about? Give **two** details.

_____

_____

3. What are the name and the telephone number of the caller?

   Name: _____

   Telephone Number: _____

4. The phonecall is to:
   (a) a library.
   (b) a police station.
   (c) hospital.
   (d) a school.

   Indicate your answer by putting **a, b, c** or **d** in the box provided. ☐

Third Part
CD3 Track 4

You will now hear a conversation between two people. The dialogue will be played **three** times, with a pause after each playing.

1. (i) Herr Hansen wishes to speak to Frau Vogt. Who is she?

      _____

      _____

   (ii) Give **one** further detail about Frau Vogt.

      _____

2. Where exactly has the graffiti been found?

   _____

   _____

   _____

3. Mention **two** reasons why Herr Hansen is so annoyed.

   _____

   _____

4. The solution suggested to the problem is:

   (a) to get the Art class to paint the wall as a project, including the graffiti.
   (b) to repaint the wall immediately.
   (c) to find out who the culprits are.
   (d) to simply leave the graffiti on the wall.

   Indicate your answer by putting **a, b, c** or **d** in the box provided. ☐

Fourth Part

You will now hear **four** news items taken from the radio, followed by the weather forecast. The news will be played **three** times; the first time right through, then in five segments with pauses, and finally right through again.

(Item 1)   `CD3 Track 5`

1. (i)   What areas must the police keep a close watch on?

_____

_____

    (ii) How many incidents were registered up to April?

_____

(Item 2)   `CD3 Track 6`

2. (i)   Who is eligible to enter the competition?

_____

    (ii) What form can the competition entries take? Mention **two** forms.

_____

_____

(Item 3)   `CD3 Track 7`

3. How many people were killed and how many were injured in the bank raid?

_____

_____

(Item 4)   `CD3 Track 8`

4. (i)   How many extremists were involved in the attack in Chemnitz?

_____

    (ii) What age were the attackers and how much damage was caused?

Age: _____

Damage: _____

(Item 5)   `CD3 Track 9`

5. Weather Forecast

    (i)   What type of weather is forecast for today? Mention **two** details.

_____

_____

    (ii) What kind of weather is forecast for the next day?

_____

_____

Wortschatz

besuchen – *to attend/to visit*
bestehen – *to pass*
durchfallen – *to fail*
das Fach (Fächer) – *subject(s)*
das Pflichtfach – *compulsory subject*
das Wahlfach – *optional subject*
die Arbeit(-en) – *test(s)*
die Note(n) – *grade(s)*
das Abitur – *Leaving Certificate*
die Schulordnung – *school rules*
die Schulpflicht – *compulsory schooling*
die Prüfung – *examination*
das Zeugnis(-se) – *school report*
die Zensur(-en) – *grade*
der Lehrplan – *syllabus*
sitzenbleiben – *to stay back*
pauken – *to swot/to work hard*
büffeln – *to swot/to work hard*

Test 16

German – Ordinary Level
LISTENING COMPREHENSION

First Part

CD3 Track 12

Listen to the CD. The interview will be played **three** times – the second time with pauses.

1. (i)   How many pupils in total attend the Heinrich-Heyne-Gymnasium?

    _____

    (ii) Name the town and Federal State in which this school is situated.

    _____

    _____

2. School for the 180 'sports pupils' and for all other pupils is the same in many ways. Mention **two** of these similarities.

_____

_____

3. (i) 'Sports pupils' at the Heinrich-Heyne-Gymnasium may engage in many types of sport. Mention any **two** of these.

_____

_____

(ii) When and how often do they train?

_____

4. What, according to Herr Weber, is the key to the success of the school?

_____

5. It is expensive to run this school. Where does the money to run it come from?

_____

Second Part

CD3 Track 13

You will now hear a telephone conversation **three** times. The secretary takes a message from the caller.

1. (i) Who does the caller wish to complain about?

_____

(ii) How did the caller hear about the incident?

_____

2. What is the cause of the caller's complaint? Give **two** details.

_____

_____

3. What are the name and the phone number of the caller?

Name: _____

Phone Number: _____

4. The phonecall is to:
   (a) a hotel.
   (b) a grocery shop.
   (c) a school.
   (d) a youth centre.

Indicate your answer by putting **a, b, c** or **d** in the box provided. ☐

Third Part

`CD3 Track 14`

You will now hear a conversation between two people. The dialogue will be played **three** times, with a pause after each playing.

1. (i)   What is Stephanie doing when Martina interrupts her to talk about her idea?

    _____

    _____

    (ii) What did Martina spot yesterday in town? Give details

    _____

    _____

2. What is the relationship between Stephanie and Martina?

    _____

3. Martina suggests that they should both wear identical outfits. Why should they do this? Give **two** reasons.

    _____

    _____

4. The idea Stephanie comes up with for the following week is:
    (a) to save the money outfits would have cost and to have a weekend away.
    (b) to buy identical outfits and to wear them to their graduation ball.
    (c) to buy identical outfits and go to the party with each other's boyfriend for a joke.
    (d) to buy their boyfriends a new outfit.

    Indicate your answer by putting **a, b, c** or **d** in the box provided.   ☐

Fourth Part

You will now hear **four** news items taken from the radio, followed by the weather forecast. The news will be played **three** times; the first time right through, then in five segments with pauses, and finally right through again.

(Item 1)

`CD3 Track 15`

1. (i)   According to the study, what percentage of pupils attend a school below their achievement level?

    _____

    (ii) How many students were surveyed as part of the study?

    _____

    _____

(Item 2)   `CD3 Track 16`

2. (i)   When will the anti-smoking law come into effect in Bremen?

_____

(ii)   In what public places in Bremen will smoking be prohibited?
Mention **two** places.

_____

_____

(Item 3)   `CD3 Track 17`

3. (i)   Name **two** states mentioned in the news item.

_____

_____

(ii)   How long are motorists being delayed at the border crossing to Salzburg?

_____

(Item 4)   `CD3 Track 18`

4. (i)   Mention any **one** effect of sending children to school too early.

_____

(ii)   According to the research, what do teachers tend to forget in relation to such children.

_____

(Item 5)   `CD3 Track 19`

5. Weather Forecast
What type of weather is forecast:
(i)   for today? Mention **two** details.

_____

_____

(ii)   for tomorrow? Mention **two** details.

_____

_____

Revision 8

CD4

1. Numbers.
   Translate the **ten** number phrases mentioned on the CD.

   _____   _____

   _____   _____

   _____   _____

   _____   _____

   _____   _____

2. Titles.
   Translate the **ten** titles mentioned on the CD.

   _____   _____

   _____   _____

   _____   _____

   _____   _____

   _____   _____

3. German cities.
   List the names of the **ten** German cities mentioned on the CD.

   _____   _____

   _____   _____

   _____   _____

   _____   _____

   _____   _____

4. At the lost and found.
   Translate the **ten** items mentioned on the CD.

   _____   _____

   _____   _____

   _____   _____

   _____   _____

5. Write down the **ten** words spelled out on the CD.

   _____   _____

   _____   _____

   _____   _____

   _____   _____

   _____   _____

Wortschatz

die Sprache(-n) – *language(s)*
die Fremdsprache(-n) – *foreign language*
die Muttersprache(-n) – *native language*
die Alltagssprache – *everyday language*
die Umgangssprache – *colloquial language*
die Aussprache – *pronunciation*
die Grammatik – *grammar*
sprachbegabt – *having a talent for languages*
die Redewendung(-en) – *idiom(s)/phrase(s)*
fließend – *fluent(ly)*
die Sprache beherrschen – *to master the language*
die Betonung – *stress*
der Kurs(-e) – *course*
unterrichten – *to teach*
der Lehrer(-) – *(male) teacher*
die Lehrerin(-nen) – *(female) teacher*
die Vokabel(-n) – *word/vocabulary item*

Test 17

German – Ordinary Level

LISTENING COMPREHENSION

First Part

CD3 Track 22

Listen to the CD. The interview will be played **three** times – the second time with pauses.

1. (i)   Susi is not particularly happy with her studies at present. What subject is she
       unhappy about?

   _____

   (ii) Give **one** reason for this.

   _____

2. Mention **two** reasons why Susi prefers her second subject.

   _____

   _____

3. Name the **two** jobs Susi considers herself capable of doing if she leaves university now.

   _____

   _____

4. Where is Günther hoping to work next year? Give **two** details.

   _____

   _____

5. (i)   Where can Susi get the application forms?

   _____

   (ii) By what date must applications be in?

   _____

Second Part

CD3 Track 23

You will now hear a telephone conversation **three** times. The receptionist takes a message from the caller.

1. What is the purpose of the call?

   _____

   _____

2. Mention any **two** details about the son's course.

   _____

   _____

3. What are the surname and the phone number of the caller?

   Surname: _____

   Phone Number: _____

4. The phonecall is to:
   (a) a secondary school.
   (b) a university.
   (c) an embassy.
   (d) a language school.

   Indicate your answer by putting **a, b, c** or **d** in the box provided. ☐

Third Part
CD3 Track 24

You will now hear a conversation between two people. The dialogue will be played **three** times, with a pause after each playing.

1. (i)   Which examination do Karl and Anna have coming up next year?

    _____

    (ii) What does Anna say about her career guidance teacher? Give **two** details.

    _____

    _____

2. (i)   Mention **two** ways in which Kai's career guidance teacher has helped him?

    _____

    _____

    (ii) Where does Anna obtain information on career choices? Give **two** sources.

    _____

    _____

3. Mention **two** questions to which Anna would like answers.

    _____

    _____

4. Towards the end of the conversation, Kai offers to help Anna by:
    (a) giving her books from the library.
    (b) letting her use his computer.
    (c) asking his career guidance teacher to help her.
    (d) dropping by with a bottle of wine.

    Indicate your answer by putting **a, b, c** or **d** in the box provided.   ☐

Fourth Part

You will now hear **four** news items taken from the radio, followed by the weather forecast. The news will be played **three** times; the first time right through, then in five segments with pauses, and finally right through again.

(Item 1)
CD3 Track 25

1. (i)   Against which immigrants (*Zuwanderer*) does the FPD chairman want sanctions introduced?

    _____

    (ii) How does he justify his demand?

    _____

(Item 2) CD3 Track 26

2. (i) What has been criticised by the chairman of the Teachers' Association?

_____

_____

(ii) According to the chairman, what are the reasons for the failings of primary schools? Mention any **one**.

_____

(Item 3) CD3 Track 27

3. (i) Give **two** details of the _Fremdsprachen_ competition.

_____

_____

(ii) According to the Minister of Education, what are the benefits of foreign languages? Mention any **one**.

_____

(Item 4) CD3 Track 28

4. (i) When does the Network Project take place?

_____

(ii) Give **two** details of the Network Project.

_____

_____

(Item 5) CD3 Track 29

5. Weather Forecast

(i) What kind of weather is forecast for today? Mention **two** details.

_____

_____

(ii) What kind of weather is expected in mountainous regions tomorrow? Mention **two** details.

_____

_____

Wortschatz

die Umwelt – *environment*
umweltbewusst – *environmentally aware*
zerstören – *to destroy*
der Umweltschutz – *environmental protection*
die Luft – *air*
die Verschmutzung – *pollution*
die globale Erwärmung – *global warming*
der steigende Meeresspiegel – *rising sea level*
der Gletscher(-) – *glacier*
schmelzen – *to melt*
das Kohlendioxid – *carbon dioxide*
der Müll – *rubbish*
sortieren – *to sort*
recyceln – *to recycle*
verbieten – *to ban*
die Tierart(-en) – *animal species*
der Lebensraum(-räume) – *habitat(s)*
zerstören – *to destroy*
aussterben – *to die out/to become extinct*
die Zukunft – *future*
die Solarenergie – *solar energy*
die Windenergie – *wind energy*

Test 18

German – Ordinary Level

LISTENING COMPREHENSION

First Part

CD3 Track 32

Listen to the CD. The interview will be played **three** times – the second time with pauses.

1. (i) Jens introduces himself at the beginning of the interview. Give **two** details about him.

   _____

   _____

   (ii) What is the aim of the group to which he belongs?

   _____

2. (i) Why did Jens and the other members think that there was a need for this group? Mention **two** details.

   _____

   _____

   (ii) Their target in the first year is to reduce the amount of rubbish by:

   (a) a quarter.
   (b) a half.
   (c) 100%.

   Indicate your answer by putting **a**, **b**, or **c** in the box provided. ☐

3. What explanation does Jens give for the large amount of packaging in the rubbish bins? Give **two** details.

   _____

   _____

4. (i) Apart from packaging, what other concerns do Jens and his group have? Mention any **one**.

   _____

   (ii) Mention the statistical findings that Jens quotes to support his concerns.

   _____

   _____

5. (i) Mention **two** measures that Jens and his group intend introducing to achieve their targets.

   _____

   _____

   (ii) Jens and his group have already had some success. Mention **one** detail.

   _____

Second Part

CD3 Track 33

You will now hear a telephone conversation **three** times. The official takes a message from the caller.

1. What is the purpose of the woman's phonecall?

   _____

   _____

2. Mention any **two** items that the caller claims she saw in the woods.

   _____

   _____

3. What are the name and phone number of the caller?

   Name: _____

   Phone Number: _____

4. At the end of the conversation, the woman agrees:
   (a) to lead an official to a place in the woods.
   (b) to go to the police.
   (c) to clean up the woods.
   (d) to ask her neighbours for help.

   Indicate your answer by putting **a, b, c** or **d** in the box provided. ☐

Third Part

CD3 Track 34

You will now hear a conversation between Lars and Frau Bergmann. The dialogue will be played **three** times, with a pause after each playing. Answer in English.

1. Lars and Frau Bergmann know each other well. Find **two** indications in the conversation to support this.

   _____

   _____

2. Why is Frau Bergmann annoyed about the condition of the skater ramp?

   _____

   _____

3. According to Lars, what is the likely cause of the problem?

   _____

   _____

4. Lars surprises Frau Bergmann by:
   (a) approaching the park warden.
   (b) going skating as if nothing had happened.
   (c) doing something practical about the problem.
   (d) walking off with his friends to a party.

   Indicate your answer by putting **a, b, c** or **d** in the box provided.

Fourth Part

You will now hear **four** news items taken from the radio, followed by the weather forecast. The news will be played **three** times; the first time right through, then in five segments with pauses, and finally right through again.

(Item 1)   CD3 Track 35

1. (i) According to the environmental organisation who in particular is in danger?

   (ii) What items should be bought with caution? Mention any **two**.

(Item 2)   CD3 Track 36

2. (i) According to scientists, by how much has the ozone layer been depleted?

   (ii) What could increase as a result?

(Item 3)   CD3 Track 37

3. (i) Which countries took part in the North Sea Conference in London?

   (ii) According to the German Minister for the Environment, what industry is at risk?

(Item 4)

4. (i) What warning has been issued by the Department of the Environment? Give **two** details.

_____

_____

(ii) What effect will this have on drivers? Give **two** details.

_____

_____

(Item 5)

5. Weather Forecast
   (i) What kind of weather is expected today? Mention **two** details.

_____

_____

(ii) What kind of weather is expected tonight? Give **two** details.

_____

_____

Wortschatz

feiern – *to celebrate*
die Geburt Christi – *the birth of Christ*
die Weihnachtszeit – *Christmas time*
die Weihnachtskarte(-n) – *Christmas card*
Frohe Weihnachten! – *Happy Christmas!*
der Kuchen – *cake*
das Christkind – *Christ child*
der Weihnachtsmarkt(-märkte) – *Christmas fair*
der Nikolaus – *Santa*
der Weihnachtsmann – *Santa*
der Baum (Bäume) – *tree*
aufstellen – *to put up*
die (Weihnachts-)Gans – *goose*
der Truthahn – *turkey*
schmücken – *to decorate*
der Christbaumschmuck – *tree decorations*
das Geschenk(-e) – *present/gift*
der Lebkuchen – *gingerbread*
der Christstollen – *Christmas log*
der Glühwein – *mulled wine*
der Heiligabend – *Christmas Eve*
der Festbraten – *festive roast*
die Bescherung – *exchange of gifts*
die Kugel(-n) – *bauble*
die Kerze(-n) – *candle*
das Weihnachtslied(-er) – *Christmas hymn*

Test 19

German – Ordinary Level

LISTENING COMPREHENSION

First Part

CD3 Track 42

Listen to the CD. The interview will be played **three** times – the second time with pauses.

1. During what period does the *Nürnberger Christkindlesmarkt* take place?

   _____

   _____

2. List **three** items that can be bought at the *Christkindlesmarkt*.

   _____

   _____

   _____

3. Describe a speciality available at the *Christkindlesmarkt* that can be consumed while there.

   _____

4. How long has the *Nürnberger Christkindlesmarkt* been in existence?

   _____

5. Mention **two** places where a similar *Christkindlesmarkt* is held?

   _____

   _____

Second Part

CD3 Track 43

You will now hear a telephone conversation **three** times. The receptionist takes a message from the caller.

1. Who does the caller wish to speak to?

   _____

2. Mention any **two** mistakes which the caller wishes to rectify.

   _____

   _____

3. What are the surname and phone number of the caller?

   Surname: _____

   Phone Number: _____

4. (i) The caller wants:
      (a) compensation sent.
      (b) an appointment with Herr Zimmermann.
      (c) Herr Zimmermann to visit him.
      (d) Herr Zimmermann to ring him back.

      Indicate your answer by putting **a**, **b**, **c** or **d** in the box provided. ☐

Third Part

CD3 Track 44

You will now hear a conversation between two people. The dialogue will be played **three** times, with a pause after each playing. Answer in English.

1. Katja is not looking forward to Christmas. Find **two** indications in the conversation to support this.

   _____

   _____

2. Mention any **two** positive things that Tim has to say about Christmas.

   _____

   _____

3. How would Katja prefer to spend Christmas? Give **two** details.

   _____

   _____

4. Tim tries to cheer up Katja by:
   (a) buying her a Christmas present.
   (b) inviting her to his house on Christmas Day.
   (c) organising an outing and party with friends on St Stephen's Day.
   (d) going away on holidays with her over Christmas.

   Indicate your answer by putting **a**, **b**, **c** or **d** in the box provided. [ ]

Fourth Part

You will now hear **four** news items taken from the radio, followed by the weather forecast. The news will be played **three** times; the first time right through, then in five segments with pauses, and finally right through again.

(Item 1)

CD3 Track 45

1. (i) Mention any **two** consequences of the house fires that happened over Christmas.

   _____

   _____

   (ii) What is thought to have caused the fire in Hamburg?

   _____

   _____

(Item 2) CD3 Track 46

2.   (i)   How many visitors came to the *Christkindlesmarkt*?

     (ii)   Mention any **one** detail of the parade (*Umzug*).

(Item 3) CD3 Track 47

3.   (i)   What kind of weather did Germany experience over the Christmas period?

     (ii)   Mention any **two** consequences arising as a result of the weather conditions.

(Item 4) CD3 Track 48

4.   (i)   How did the Zurich police manage to track a burglar?

     (ii)   How far did the thief live from the shop he had burgled?

(Item 5) CD3 Track 49

5.   Weather Forecast
     (i)   What weather conditions are expected in Germany today? Give any **two** details.

     (ii)   What is the forecast for tomorrow? Give any **two** details.

Wortschatz

die Wohngemeinschaft – *house share*
die Unkosten – *expenses*
die Hausordnung – *the house rules*
die Miete – *rent*
der/die Mieter/-in – *tenant*
der/die Vermieter/-in – *landlord*
die Kaution – *deposit*
zahlen – *to pay*
die Heizung – *heating*
der Strom – *electricity*
selbständig – *independent*
das Studentenwohnheim – *student accommodation*
das Privatleben – *privacy*

Test 20

German – Ordinary Level

LISTENING COMPREHENSION

First Part

CD3 Track 52

Listen to the CD. The interview will be played **three** times – the second time with pauses.

1. (i) Why was Erika not able to contact Stefan?

    _____

    _____

   (ii) In which subject did Erika have an examination that day?

    _____

2. (i) At what time was Erika to meet her professor?

    _____

   (ii) What percentage of the examination was awarded for the report?

    _____

3. (i) What proposal has Stefan for Erika? Give details.

_____

_____

(ii) Why is the house only available until June?

_____

4. Mention any **two** costs associated with Stefan's proposal.

_____

_____

5. (i) From what date will they be able to avail of the opportunity?

_____

(ii) What difficulty does Erika have with Stefan's proposal?

_____

_____

Second Part

CD3 Track 53

You will now hear a telephone conversation **three** times. The receptionist takes a message from the caller.

1. What is the purpose of the call?

_____

_____

2. Mention any **three** items listed by the caller as missing.

_____

_____

_____

3. What are the surname and phone number of the caller?

Surname: _____

Phone Number: _____

4. The caller is calling:
   (a) an insurance company.
   (b) a police station.
   (c) a lost property office.
   (d) a jewellery shop.

Indicate your answer by putting **a, b, c** or **d** in the box provided. ☐

Third Part

CD3 Track 54

You will now hear a conversation between two people. The dialogue will be played **three** times, with a pause after each playing. Answer in English.

1. Why does Silke want to move into her own flat? Give **two** reasons.

   _____

   _____

2. Why does her father not want her to move out? Give **two** reasons.

   _____

   _____

3. How does Silke hope to finance her own flat? Mention **two** sources of money she considers.

   _____

   _____

4. At the end of the conversation, Silke decides to:
   (a) not do the Leaving Certificate (*Abitur*).
   (b) stay with her parents for another few years.
   (c) get a part-time job and move out after the *Abitur*.
   (d) ask her mother for money.

   Indicate your answer by putting **a**, **b**, **c** or **d** in the box provided. ☐

Fourth Part

You will now hear **four** news items taken from the radio, followed by the weather forecast. The news will be played **three** times; the first time right through, then in five segments with pauses, and finally right through again.

(Item 1)

CD3 Track 55

1. Give **two** reasons why was it so easy for the thieves to break into and rob the house in Braunschweig.

   _____

   _____

(Item 2)

CD3 Track 56

2. Using plastic is a new design trend.
   (i) What product is now made of plastic?

   _____

   _____

(ii) Give **two** advantages mentioned for its use.

_____

_____

(Item 3) CD3 Track 57

3. (i) According to the bulletin, what is the cause of the disaster in northern California?

_____

_____

(ii) Mention any **two** effects of the disaster.

_____

_____

(Item 4) CD3 Track 58

4. (i) What kind of catastrophe was reported from Turkey?

_____

_____

(ii) Give **two** details of the damage caused.

_____

_____

(Item 5) CD3 Track 59

5. Weather Forecast
   (i) What kind of weather is expected for tomorrow? Give **two** details.

_____

_____

(ii) What is causing the traffic-jam on the A8?

_____

_____

Higher Level

Aural Comprehension

Einheit 1

Wortschatz

das Alter – *old age*
die Rente – *pension*
der Rentner/die Rentnerin – *pensioner*
Senioren – *senior citizens*
das Seniorenheim – *old folks home*
die Gesellschaft – *company/society*
das Enkelkind (-er) – *grandchild*
die Einsamkeit – *loneliness*
die Isolierung – *isolation*
Probleme der Gesundheit – *health problems*
besuchen – *to visit*
pensioniert – *retired*
im Ruhestand sein – *to be retired*
einkaufen gehen – *to go shopping*
sauber machen – *to clean*
reden mit ihnen – *to talk to them*
ihnen Gesellschaft leisten – *to keep them company*

Test 1

German – Higher Level
LISTENING COMPREHENSION

First Part

CD1 Track 2

The interview will be played three times: first right through, then in segments with pauses, and finally right through again.

1. Why is Laura so frustrated? Explain giving **two** details.

   _____

   _____

2. Michael describes a particular scheme:
   (i) What is the title of the scheme?

   _____

(ii) Explain how the scheme works, mentioning **three** details.

_____

_____

_____

3. What kind of help does Michael's landlord need?
    Explain why, giving **three** details.

_____

_____

_____

4. Why could Michael not move in immediately?

_____

_____

5. At the end of the conversation, Laura and Michael both agree that the *Wohnen für Hilfe* scheme is an excellent one. Mention any **two** advantages they see in it.

_____

_____

_____

Second Part

CD1 Track 3

You will now hear a telephone conversation. The receptionist takes a message from the caller.

To allow you to answer **Question 1** (the note), the phonecall will be played **twice**, with a pause after each playing during which you should **fill in the box**. The phonecall will then be played for a third and final time to allow you to answer **Question 2** (the **language** of the phonecall).

1. Write out **in German** the note which the receptionist will leave.
    (**Key words, not full sentences**)
    The note should contain:
    - whom the caller wishes to speak to.
    - name of caller.
    - problem caller wishes to discuss.
    - message regarding further contact.
    - telephone number of caller.

Anruf für: _____

Anruf von: _____

Nachricht (stichwortartig):
Problem: _____

_____

Der Anrufer:

☐ möchte einen Termin für morgen Nachmittag.

☐ wird heute Nachmittag angerufen werden.

☐ erhält morgen Nachmittag einen Anruf.

☐ ruft morgen Nachmittag zurück.

Kontaktnummer: _____

Now answer Question 2.

2. After listening to the phonecall for the third time, pick out **three** examples of the language (**expressions and phrases, not tone of voice**) used in the phonecall that show the caller's **annoyance**.

_____

_____

_____

Third Part

CD1 Track 4

You will now hear a conversation between two people. The dialogue will be played **three** times, with a pause after each playing. Answer in English.

1. (i) The conversation is between:
    (a) a teacher and a pupil.
    (b) a policeman and a pickpocket.
    (c) an employer and a person doing voluntary work.
    (d) two colleagues at work.

    Indicate your choice by putting **a, b, c** or **d** in the box provided. ☐

(ii) Find **two** indications in the conversation to support your choice.

_____

_____

2. (i)   Which adjective best describes Herr Lehmann's attitude during the conversation?
          (a) stressed out
          (b) rude
          (c) indifferent
          (d) bored

          Indicate your choice by putting **a, b, c** or **d** in the box provided. ☐

    (ii) Write down **two** details from the conversation to support your choice.

          _____

          _____

3. (i)   What arguments does Frau Adam use during the conversation? Give details.

          _____

          _____

          _____

    (ii) What decision does Herr Lehmann come to at the end of the conversation? Give details.

          _____

          _____

          _____

Fourth Part

You will now hear **four** news items taken from the radio, followed by the weather forecast. The news will be played **three** times; the first time right through, then in five segments with pauses, and finally right through again.

(Item 1)   CD1 Track 5
1. (i)   How much money was involved and who was the victim?

          _____

    (ii) How did the employee steal the money? Give details.

          _____

          _____

(Item 2)   CD1 Track 6
2. (i)   What is the main finding of the study carried out among pensioners?

          _____

(ii)   Mention any **two** reasons given for the finding.

_____

_____

(Item 3)
CD1 Track 7

3. (i)   According to the EU survey, what are the **two** things of most concern to pensioners?

_____

_____

(ii)   Give **two** details about those who were surveyed.

_____

_____

(Item 4)
CD1 Track 8

4. (i)   Where did the attack described here take place?

_____

(ii)   Give **three** details of what happened to the victim.

_____

_____

_____

(Item 5)
CD1 Track 9

5. Weather Forecast
What type of weather is forecast:
(i)   for today?

_____

_____

(ii)   for the next day?

_____

_____

Ausländer

Einheit 2

2

Wortschatz

der Ausländer(-) – *foreigner(s)*
der Immigrant(-en) – *immigrant(s)*
Arbeit suchen – *to look for work*
der Flüchtling(-e) – *refugee(s)*
der Rassismus – *racism*
flüchten – *to flee*
die Hautfarbe – *skin colour*
die Heimat – *homeland*
das Ausland – *abroad*
die Sprache – *language*
die Toleranz – *tolerance*
die Qualifikation (-en) – *qualification(s)*
die Sozialhilfe – *social welfare*
das Vorurteil(-e) – *prejudice*
die Kultur(-en) – *culture(s)*
integriert werden – *to become integrated*
der Unterschied(e) – *difference*
leben und leben lassen – *to live and let live*
akzeptieren – *to accept*
die Festung Europa – *Fortress Europe*

Test 2

German – Higher Level
LISTENING COMPREHENSION

First Part   CD1 Track 12

The interview will be played **three** times: first right through, then in segments with pauses, and finally right through again.

1. (i)   Where does Herr Özkan work? Give details.

    _____

    (ii) How long has he been living in Germany?

    _____

2. What was the extent of Herr Özkan's knowledge of German when he first arrived in Germany?

_____

3. (i) What problems did Herr Özkan face when he started school?

_____

   (ii) Why did he not wish to go to college? Give **two** details.

_____

_____

4. (i) What did Herr Özkan do immediately after he left school?

_____

_____

   (ii) What other jobs did he do before he settled into his current job? Give details.

_____

_____

_____

5. What are Herr Özkan's plans for the future? Mention **three** details.

_____

_____

_____

Second Part

CD1 Track 13

You will now hear a telephone conversation. The secretary takes a message from the caller.

To allow you to answer **Question 1 (the note)**, the phonecall will be played **twice**, with a pause after each playing during which you should **fill in the box**. The phonecall will then be played for a third and final time to allow you to answer **Question 2 (the language** of the phonecall).

1. Write out **in German** the note which the secretary will leave.
   (Key words, not full sentences)
   The note should contain:
   - whom the caller wishes to speak to.
   - name of caller.
   - problem caller wishes to discuss.
   - message regarding further contact.
   - telephone number of caller.

Anruf für: _____

Anruf von: _____

Nachricht (stichwortartig):
Problem: _____

_____

Der Anrufer:

- [ ] möchte einen Termin für morgen Nachmittag.
- [ ] wird heute Nachmittag angerufen werden.
- [ ] erhält morgen Nachmittag einen Anruf.
- [ ] ruft morgen Nachmittag zurück.

Kontaktnummer: _____

Now answer Question 2.

2. After listening to the phonecall for the third time, pick out **three** examples of the language (**expressions and phrases, not tone of voice**) used in the phonecall that show the caller's **worried state**.

_____

_____

_____

Third Part

CD1 Track 14

You will now hear a conversation between two people. The dialogue will be played **three** times, with a pause after each playing. Answer in English.

1. (i) The conversation is between:
   (a) a teacher and a pupil.
   (b) two pupils.
   (c) a brother and sister.
   (d) two teachers.

   Indicate your choice by putting **a, b, c** or **d** in the box provided. [ ]

   (ii) Find **two** indications in the conversation to support your choice.

   _____

   _____

2. (i) Which adjective best describes Fatima's attitude during the conversation?
  (a) stressed out
  (b) dissatisfied
  (c) indifferent
  (d) bored

  Indicate your choice by putting **a**, **b**, **c** or **d** in the box provided.

  (ii) Write down **two** details from the conversation to support your choice.

  _____

  _____

3. (i) What suggestions does Bastian make? Give details.

  _____

  _____

  (ii) What does Fatima decide to do at the end of the conversation?

  _____

  _____

Fourth Part

You will now hear **four** news items taken from the radio, followed by the weather forecast. The news will be played three times; the first time right through, then in five segments with pauses, and finally right through again.

(Item 1)   CD1 Track 15
1. (i) Give details of the incident reported here.

  _____

  _____

  (ii) Who was the victim?

  _____

  _____

(Item 2)   CD1 Track 16
2. (i) Give details of the family involved in the item.

  _____

  _____

(ii) How had the thief managed to steal the item? Give details.

_____

_____

(Item 3)   **CD1 Track 17**

3. (i) What must foreigners of German origin do before they will be allowed to move to Germany?

_____

_____

(ii) How many people applied for permission to move to Germany the previous year?

_____

_____

(Item 4)   **CD1 Track 18**

4. (i) What is causing concern to the Federal government?

_____

_____

(ii) What statistics are used to back up the concern?

_____

_____

(Item 5)   **CD1 Track 19**

5. Weather Forecast
   (i) What type of weather is expected? Give details.

_____

_____

(ii) What kind of weather is forecast for the weekend?

_____

_____

Revision 1

1. List the **ten** numbers mentioned on the CD.

    _____   _____

    _____   _____

    _____   _____

    _____   _____

    _____   _____

2. Food.
    Translate the **ten** food items mentioned on the CD.

    _____   _____

    _____   _____

    _____   _____

    _____   _____

    _____   _____

3. Scenery.
    Name the **ten** types of scenery mentioned on the CD.

    _____   _____

    _____   _____

    _____   _____

    _____   _____

    _____   _____

4. Germany.
    List the **ten** geographical items mentioned on the CD.

    _____   _____

    _____   _____

    _____   _____

    _____   _____

    _____   _____

5. List the **five** names spelled out on the CD.

    _____

    _____

    _____

    _____

    _____

Wortschatz

der Austausch – *exchange*
der/die Austauschpartner/-in – *exchange partner*
Deutschkenntnisse (pl.) – *knowledge of German*
aufbessern – *to improve*
die Alltagssprache – *everyday language*
auskommen mit (+ Dat.) – *to get on with*
der Deutschkurs(e) – *German course(s)*
bei einer Familie – *with a family*
Sitten und Gebräuche kennen lernen – *to get to know customs and traditions*
die gesprochene Sprache – *the spoken language*
die Redewendung(-en) – *phrases/idioms*
die Einheimischen – *the natives*
Dialekt(e) – *dialect*
seine Horizonte erweitern – *to broaden one's horizons*
andere Länder, andere Sitten – *different countries, different customs*
die Globalisierung – *globalisation*
eine andere Mentalität – *a different mentality*

Test 3

German – Higher Level

LISTENING COMPREHENSION

First Part

CD1 Track 22

The interview will be played **three** times: first right through, then in segments with pauses, and finally right through again.

1. (i) When did Detlef Soitzek start the High Seas High School project in Germany, and what was his role?

   _____

   (ii) Who was his partner in starting the project?

   _____

2. (i) When does the project take place each year, and how long does it last?

_____

_____

_____

(ii) Who else is on board the ship? Give **three** details.

_____

_____

_____

3. (i) Mention **five** subjects taught on board ship.

_____

_____

_____

_____

_____

(ii) Give **two** examples of projects the pupils get involved in on dry land.

_____

_____

4. Mention **two** of the regular chores to be done on the _Thor Heyerdahl_.

_____

_____

5. What proves that the students have learned a lot about sailing during the voyage? Give details.

_____

_____

_____

_____

_____

Second Part

CD1 Track 23

You will now hear a telephone conversation. The receptionist takes a message from the caller.

To allow you to answer **Question 1 (the note)**, the phonecall will be played **twice**, with a pause after each playing during which you should **fill in the box**. The phonecall will then be played for a third and final time to allow you to answer **Question 2** (the **language** of the phonecall).

1. Write out **in German** the note which the receptionist will leave.
    (Key words, not full sentences)
    The note should contain:
    - whom the caller wishes to speak to.
    - name of caller.
    - problem caller wishes to discuss.
    - message regarding further contact.
    - telephone number of caller.

Anruf von: _____

Anruf für: _____

Nachricht (stichwortartig):
Problem: _____

_____

Der Anrufer:
- ☐ ruft später zurück.
- ☐ wird zurückgerufen.
- ☐ kommt in zwei Stunden vorbei.
- ☐ kommt in einer halben Stunde vorbei.

Telefonnummer des Anrufers: _____

Now answer Question 2.
2. After listening to the phonecall for the third time, pick out **three** examples of the language (**expressions and phrases, not tone of voice**) used in the phonecall that show the caller's **annoyance**.

_____

_____

_____

Third Part

CD1 Track 24

You will now hear a conversation between two people. The dialogue will be played **three** times, with a pause after each playing. Answer in English.

1. (i)   The conversation is between:
    (a) two babysitters.
    (b) two hikers.
    (c) two exchange students.
    (d) two classmates.

    Indicate your choice by putting **a**, **b**, **c** or **d** in the box provided.

    (ii) Find **two** indications in the conversation to support your choice.

    _____

    _____

2. (i)   Which adjective best describes Salome's reaction during the conversation?
    (a) angry
    (b) nervous
    (c) jealous
    (d) fed up

    Indicate your choice by putting **a**, **b**, **c** or **d** in the box provided.

    (ii) Write down **two** details from the conversation to support your choice.

    _____

    _____

3. (i)   What practical advice does Ingo give Salome as a possible solution to her problem? Give details.

    _____

    _____

    (ii) What is Salome's plan for next year's holiday?

    _____

    _____

Fourth Part

You will now hear **four** news items taken from the radio, followed by the weather forecast. The news will be played **three** times; the first time right through, then in five segments with pauses, and finally right through again.

(Item 1)   CD1 Track 25

1. (i)   Who was killed in the accident?

_____

_____

(ii)   Give details of when and how the accident happened.

_____

_____

(Item 2)   CD1 Track 26

2. (i)   How many journalists died while reporting last year?

_____

_____

(ii)   What were the main causes of death? Mention any **two**.

_____

_____

(Item 3)   CD1 Track 27

3. Give details of the kidnapping in Columbia.

_____

_____

_____

(Item 4)   CD1 Track 28

4. (i)   What is the cause of the traffic problems at this time?

_____

_____

(ii)   Where are the problems at their worst? Give details.

_____

_____

_____

(Item 5)

CD1 Track 29

5. Weather Forecast

What type of weather is forecast:

(i)   for today?

_____

_____

(ii) for the next few days?

_____

_____

Wortschatz

das Auto(s) – *car*
der Zug (Züge) – *train*
die Bahn – *rail*
die Straßenbahn – *tram*
das Fahrrad (-räder) – *bicycle*
der/ die Fahrer/-in – *driver*
der Führerschein – *licence*
die Versicherung – *insurance*
die Erfahrung – *experience*
das Benzin – *petrol*
die Gefahr(-en) – *danger*
gefährlich – *dangerous*
die Geschwindigkeit – *speed*
rasen – *to speed*
zu schnelles Fahren – *speeding*
(die) Trunkenheit am Steuer – *drink driving*
öffentliche Verkehrsmittel (pl.) – *public (means of) transport*
der Unfall(-fälle) – *accident*
der Verkehr – *traffic*
der Stau – *traffic-jam*
praktisch – *convenient*
das Warten – *waiting*
die Unkosten – *costs*
die Umwelt – *the environment*
angeben – *to show-off*
vorschlagen – *to suggest*

Test 4

German – Higher Level
LISTENING COMPREHENSION

First Part

CD1 Track 32

The interview will be played **three** times: first right through, then in segments with pauses, and finally right through again.

1. (i)   How long has Jens been a taxi-driver?

    _____

    (ii) Driving a taxi is a sideline for Jens. Why does he work as a taxi driver?

    _____

    _____

2. Mention any **three** conditions (apart from passing a medical test) that one must fulfil
    in order to obtain a licence to drive a taxi?

    _____

    _____

    _____

3. Mention any **two** of the tests Jens had to undergo during his medical examination?

    _____

    _____

4. (i)   Jens also had to pass a written and an oral examination. What was tested in
          these examinations? Mention any **two** details (one oral and one written).

    _____

    _____

    (ii) How much did Jens have to pay?

    _____

5. (i)   What aspects of the work appeal to Jens?

    _____

    _____

    _____

    (ii) Mention any **two** aspects that he does not enjoy.

    _____

    _____

Second Part

CD1 Track 33

You will now hear a telephone conversation. The receptionist takes a message from the caller.

To allow you to answer **Question 1** (**the note**), the phonecall will be played **twice**, with a pause after each playing during which you should **fill in the box**. The phonecall will then be played for a third and final time to allow you to answer **Question 2** (the **language** of the phonecall).

1. Write out **in German** the note which the receptionist will leave.
   (**Key words, not full sentences**)
   The note should contain:
   - name of caller.
   - problem caller wishes to discuss.
   - make and number of car.
   - telephone number of caller.

Anruf von: _____

Nachricht (stichwortartig):
Problem: _____

_____

Automarke: _____ Kennzeichen: _____

Handynummer: _____

Now answer Question 2.

2. After listening to the phonecall for the third time, pick out **three** examples of the language (**expressions and phrases, not tone of voice**) used in the phonecall that show the caller's **fear**.

_____

_____

_____

Third Part

CD1 Track 34

You will now hear a conversation between two people. The dialogue will be played **three** times, with a pause after each playing. Answer in English.

1. (i)   The conversation is between:
    (a) parent and teenager.
    (b) two classmates.
    (c) two neighbouring teenagers.
    (d) two elderly neighbours.

    Indicate your choice by putting **a, b, c** or **d** in the box provided.

    (ii) Find **two** indications in the conversation to support your choice.

    _____

    _____

2. (i)   Which adjective best describes Maike's attitude during the conversation?
    (a) sarcastic
    (b) judgemental
    (c) diplomatic
    (d) indifferent

    Indicate your choice by putting **a, b, c** or **d** in the box provided.

    (ii) Give **two** details from the conversation to support your choice.

    _____

    _____

3. (i)   As the conversation goes on, Sven expresses his annoyance very directly.
    Give **three** indications of this.

    _____

    _____

    _____

    (ii) What does Maike suggest they should do in the end?

    _____

    _____

    _____

Fourth Part

You will now hear **four** news items taken from the radio, followed by the weather forecast. The news will be played **three** times; the first time right through, then in five segments with pauses, and finally right through again.

(Item 1)   `CD1 Track 35`

1. (i) Who was driving the car?

_____

(ii) What caused the accident? Give **two** reasons.

_____

_____

(Item 2)   `CD1 Track 36`

2. (i) Where is the traffic chaos at its worst?

_____

_____

_____

(ii) What gave rise to such chaos on the roads? Give details.

_____

_____

_____

(Item 3)   `CD1 Track 37`

3. (i) When and where did the accident happen?

_____

_____

(ii) What happened as a result of the accident? Give **two** details.

_____

_____

(Item 4)   `CD1 Track 38`

4. (i) List in note form the details leading up to the accident.

_____

_____

_____

    (ii) Give details of the casualties suffered.

_____

_____

_____

(Item 5)   **CD1 Track 39**

  5. Weather Forecast

    (i)   What type of weather is forecast for Sunday morning?

_____

_____

    (ii) Give details of the weather expected for Sunday afternoon.

_____

_____

Revision 2

CD4

1. List the **ten** years mentioned on the CD.

    _____   _____

    _____   _____

    _____   _____

    _____   _____

    _____   _____

2. Parts of the body.
    Translate the **ten** parts of the body mentioned on the CD.

    _____   _____

    _____   _____

    _____   _____

    _____   _____

    _____   _____

3. Weather.
    Translate the **ten** weather topics mentioned on the CD.

    _____   _____

    _____   _____

    _____   _____

    _____   _____

    _____   _____

4. Geography.
    Translate the **ten** geographical items mentioned on the CD.

    _____   _____

    _____   _____

    _____   _____

    _____   _____

    _____   _____

5. Health.
    Translate the **ten** sicknesses mentioned on the CD.

    _____   _____

    _____   _____

    _____   _____

    _____   _____

    _____   _____

Wortschatz

der Rollstuhl – *wheelchair*
die Blindheit – *blindness*
körperbehindert – *having a physical disability*
geistig behindert – *having a mental disability*
ausgeschlossen – *excluded*
die Punktschrift (Braille-Schrift) – *Braille*
breite Türeingänge – *wide doorways*
die Diskriminierung – *discrimination*
(querschnitt)gelähmt – *paralysed*
Minderwertigkeitskomplex – *inferiority complex*

Test 5

German – Higher Level
LISTENING COMPREHENSION

First Part

CD1 Track 42

The interview will be played **three** times: first right through, then in segments with pauses, and finally right through again.

1. (i) Where does Herr Treige live?

   _____

   (ii) How long has he been in a wheelchair?

   _____

2. (i) Herr Treige was involved in an accident. Mention any **three** details?

   _____

   _____

   _____

   (ii) How long did he spend in hospital?

   _____

3. What did Herr Treige do after coming out of hospital?

_____

_____

_____

4. (i) What does Herr Treige's work consist of?

_____

_____

(ii) Mention **two** things he likes about his job.

_____

_____

5. (i) What difficulties does Herr Treige encounter in his daily life?

_____

_____

(ii) What activities does he miss most?

_____

_____

Second Part

CD1 Track 43

You will now hear a telephone conversation. The receptionist takes a message from the caller.

To allow you to answer **Question 1 (the note)**, the phonecall will be played **twice,** with a pause after each playing during which you should **fill in the box.** The phonecall will then be played for a third and final time to allow you to answer **Question 2** (the **language** of the phonecall).

1. Write out **in German** the note which the receptionist will leave.
   (**Key words, not full sentences**)
   The note should contain:
   - whom the caller wishes to speak to.
   - name of caller.
   - problem caller wishes to discuss.
   - message regarding further contact.
   - telephone number of caller.
   - caller's email address.

Anruf für: _____

Anruf von: _____

Nachricht (stichwortartig):

Problem: _____

_____

Der Anrufer:

☐   möchte einen Termin für morgen Vormittag.

☐   wird heute Vormittag angerufen werden.

☐   erhält morgen Vormittag einen Anruf.

☐   ruft morgen Vormittag zurück.

Kontaktnummer: _____

Email-Adresse: _____

Now answer Question 2.

2. After listening to the phonecall for the third time, pick out **three** examples of the language (**expressions and phrases, not tone of voice**) used in the phonecall that show the receptionist's helpfulness.

_____

_____

_____

Third Part

CD1 Track 44

You will now hear a conversation between two people. The dialogue will be played **three** times, with a pause after each playing. Answer in English.

1. (i)   The conversation is between:

      (a) a teacher and a pupil.
      (b) a nurse and patient.
      (c) a doctor and nurse.
      (d) two pupils.

      Indicate your choice by putting **a, b, c** or **d** in the box provided. ☐

    (ii) Find **two** indications in the conversation to support your choice.

_____

_____

2. Which adjective best describes Julia's attitude during the conversation?
   (a) worried
   (b) confident
   (c) indifferent
   (d) bored

   Indicate your choice by putting **a, b, c** or **d** in the box provided. ☐

3. (i) Mention any **two** problems that Julia refers to.

   _____

   _____

   (ii) What suggestions does Christian make at the end? Give details.

   _____

   _____

   _____

Fourth Part

You will now hear **four** news items taken from the radio, followed by the weather forecast. The news will be played **three** times; the first time right through, then in five segments with pauses, and finally right through again.

(Item 1) `CD1 Track 45`

1. (i) The Foundation for Reading has released some surprising findings. What are these?

   _____

   _____

   (ii) Where, according to the Foundation spokesperson, does the blame lie? Mention **two** points the spokesperson makes to support the claim.

   _____

   _____

(Item 2) `CD1 Track 46`

2. (i) Describe the new initiative in Wickede, mentioning **three** details.

   _____

   _____

   _____

(ii) How much money do the families receive in payment and how much money is saved?

_____

_____

(Item 3) CD1 Track 47

3. (i) Give details of those involved in the scheme for disabled children in Hagen.

_____

_____

(ii) What services will the centre provide? Mention **three** details.

_____

_____

_____

(Item 4) CD1 Track 48

4. (i) How long has _Aktion Sorgenkind_ been in existence and who does it try to help?

_____

_____

(ii) Give examples of the help provided by _Aktion Sorgenkind_ over the years.

_____

_____

_____

(Item 5) CD1 Track 49

5. Weather Forecast
What type of weather is expected:
(i) for today? Give details.

_____

_____

(ii) for tomorrow? Mention **two** details.

_____

_____

Wortschatz

der Computer(-) – *computer*
der PC – *PC, computer*
der Laptop(-s) – *laptop*
die Maus – *mouse*
das Computerspiel(-e) – *computer game*
der Chatraum(-räume) – *chat room*
die Webseite(-n) – *web page*
der Nutzer(-) – *user(s)*
emailen – *email*
die Email – *email*
das Internet – *internet*
ins Internet gehen – *to go on the internet*
meine eigene Facebook-Seite – *my own Facebook page*
die Datei(-en) – *file*
speichern – *to save*
das Laufwerk – *driver*
die Festplatte – *hard drive*
laden – *to load*
der Drucker – *printer*

Test 6

German – Higher Level
LISTENING COMPREHENSION

First Part   CD1 Track 52

The interview will be played **three** times: first right through, then in segments with pauses, and finally right through again.

1. (i) How long has Frau Spengler been working in the post-office?

    _____

   (ii) On what date did she begin working there?

    _____

2. (i) What did a typical working day consist of? Give details.

_____

_____

_____

_____

_____

(ii) How has Eva's work changed? Mention **three** details.

_____

_____

_____

3. (i) Mention **five** items that have been recently introduced for sale in the post-office.

_____

_____

_____

_____

_____

(ii) Why is business so good? Give **two** reasons.

_____

_____

4. Why did the post-office management decide on this new venture? Give **three** details.

_____

_____

_____

5. Describe Eva's training. Mention any **two** details.

_____

_____

_____

Second Part

You will now hear a telephone conversation. The secretary of Ikea in Düsseldorf takes a message.

To allow you to answer **Question 1** (**the note**), the phonecall will be played **twice**, with a pause after each playing during which you should **fill in the box**. The phonecall will then be played for a third and final time to allow you to answer **Question 2** (the **language** of the phonecall).

1. Write out **in German** the key information that the secretary jots down as a memo. (**Key words, not full sentences**)
   The note should contain:
   - ◼ name of caller.
   - ◼ problem caller wishes to discuss.
   - ◼ details regarding further contact.
   - ◼ telephone number of caller.

Anruf für: _____

Anruf von: _____

Nachricht (stichwortartig):

Problem: _____

_____

Der Anrufer:

☐ ruft in einer halben Stunde nochmal an.
☐ bittet um einen Termin.
☐ erhält in einer halben Stunde einen Rückruf.
☐ wird sich Ende der Woche wieder melden.

Telefonnummer des Anrufers: _____

Now answer Question 2.

2. After listening to the phonecall for the third time, pick out **three** examples of the language (**expressions and phrases, not tone of voice**) used by the caller to explain his **confusion**.

_____

_____

_____

Third Part

CD1 Track 54

You will now hear a conversation between two people. The dialogue will be played **three** times, with a pause after each playing. Answer in English.

1. (i)   The conversation is between:
    (a) two doctors.
    (b) a journalist and a hospital employee.
    (c) two work colleagues.
    (d) a doctor and a nurse.

    Indicate your choice by putting **a**, **b**, **c** or **d** in the box provided. ☐

    (ii) Find **two** indications in the conversation to support your choice.

    _____

    _____

2. Which adjective best describes Herr Kux's attitude during the conversation?
    (a) stressed out
    (b) interested
    (c) indifferent
    (d) bored

    Indicate your choice by putting **a**, **b**, **c** or **d** in the box provided. ☐

3. (i)   Mention **two** details of the type of work that goes on in Peter Kux's workplace.

    _____

    _____

    (ii) Mention any **two** details of the work he does.

    _____

    _____

Fourth Part

You will now hear **four** news items taken from the radio, followed by the weather forecast. The news will be played **three** times; the first time right through, then in five segments with pauses, and finally right through again.

(Item 1)

CD1 Track 55

1. (i)   Who is invited to take part in Netdays?

    _____

    _____

(ii) Give the following details of Netdays: latest date for entry; duration of event; organiser.

_____

_____

_____

(Item 2) CD1 Track 56

2. (i) What warning has been issued by computer experts?

_____

_____

(ii) What effect does this item have?

_____

_____

(Item 3) CD1 Track 57

3. (i) What percentage of German internet users chooses not to shop online?

_____

(ii) Mention any **three** reasons why this is the case.

_____

_____

_____

(Item 4) CD1 Track 58

4. (i) Germans spend more and more money booking travel tickets online. How much money did they spend last year and in 2003?

_____

(ii) Who profits mainly from this new trend?

_____

_____

(Item 5) CD1 Track 59

5. Weather Forecast
    (i) What will weather conditions be like today?

_____

(ii) What is the forecast for tomorrow?

_____

_____

Revision 3

1. List the **ten** dates mentioned on the CD.

   _____   _____

   _____   _____

   _____   _____

   _____   _____

   _____   _____

2. Cars.
   Translate the **ten** car-related items mentioned on the CD.

   _____   _____

   _____   _____

   _____   _____

   _____   _____

   _____   _____

3. Federal states.
   List the **ten** federal states (Bundesländer) mentioned on the CD.

   _____   _____

   _____   _____

   _____   _____

   _____   _____

   _____   _____

4. List the **five** names spelled out on the CD.

   _____

   _____

   _____

   _____

   _____

5. Materials.
   Translate the **ten** materials mentioned on the CD.

   _____   _____

   _____   _____

   _____   _____

   _____   _____

Wortschatz

die Ausbeutung – *exploitation*
die Hilfsorganisation(-en) – *aid organisation*
karitative Organisation(-en) – *charitable organisation*
der Völkermord – *genocide*
spenden – *to donate*
die Spende(-n) – *donation*
die Hungersnot(-nöte) – *famine*
die Dürre(-n) – *drought*
die Kinderarbeit – *child labour*
die Sklaverei – *slavery*
der Sklave(-n) – *slave(s)*
verhungern – *to starve to death*
verdursten – *to die of thirst*
die Krankheit(-en) – *illness*
sauberes Wasser – *clean water*
der Hungerlohn – *starvation wage*
das Straßenkind(-er) – *street child*
die Überbevölkerung – *over-population*

Test 7

German – Higher Level

LISTENING COMPREHENSION

First Part

CD1 Track 62

The interview will be played **three** times: first right through, then in segments with pauses, and finally right through again.

1. (i) For how long has the Vocational School in Altötting been involved in Third World projects?

    _____

    _____

(ii) The use of solar energy for cooking has become very necessary in some parts of Africa. Mention **two** of the reasons given.

2. (i) What does a solar cooker look like as Johannes describes it?

(ii) List **three** advantages of the solar cooker.

3. How did the solar cooker project begin?

4. How many solar cookers have been made so far in Uganda?

5. Johannes held a workshop in Uganda. Give **three** details.

Second Part

CD1 Track 63

You will now hear a telephone conversation. The receptionist takes a message from the caller.

To allow you to answer **Question 1 (the note)**, the phonecall will be played **twice**, with a pause after each playing during which you should **fill in the box**. The phonecall will then be played for a third and final time to allow you to answer **Question 2 (the language** of the phonecall).

1. Write out **in German** the note that the receptionist will leave.
   (**Key words, not full sentences**)
   The note should contain:
   - name of caller.
   - matter caller wishes to discuss.
   - message regarding further contact.
   - telephone number of caller.

Anruf von: _____

Nachricht (stichwortartig):
Problem: _____

_____

Der Anrufer:
- [ ] möchte einen Termin für morgen Nachmittag.
- [ ] ruft morgen Nachmittag zurück.

Kontaktnummer: (Vorwahl) _____ (Nummer) _____

Now answer Question 2.

2. After listening to the phonecall for the third time, pick out **three** examples of the language (**expressions and phrases, not tone of voice**) used in the phonecall that show the caller's **enthusiasm**.

   _____

   _____

   _____

Third Part
CD1 Track 64

You will now hear a conversation between Frau Hoppe and Christian. The dialogue will be played **three** times, with a pause after each playing. Answer in English.

1. (i) The conversation is between:
   - (a) a married couple.
   - (b) two neighbours.
   - (c) two holiday makers.
   - (d) a teacher and a former pupil.

   Indicate your choice by putting **a**, **b**, **c** or **d** in the box provided. ☐

(ii) Find **two** indications in the conversation to support your choice.

_____

_____

2. (i) Which adjective best describes Christian's reaction during the conversation?
    (a) stressed out
    (b) content
    (c) indifferent
    (d) bored

    Indicate your choice by putting **a**, **b**, **c** or **d** in the box provided.   ☐

    (ii) Write down **two** details from the conversation to support your choice.

    _____

    _____

3. (i) What exactly did Christian do in India? Give details.

    _____

    _____

    _____

    (ii) What does the teacher suggest to Christian at the end of the conversation?

    _____

    _____

    _____

Fourth Part

You will now hear **four** news items taken from the radio, followed by the weather forecast. The news will be played **three** times; the first time right through, then in five segments with pauses, and finally right through again.

(Item 1)   CD1 Track 65

1. The charity organisation _Brot für die Welt_ is unhappy. What is the reason for this? Give details.

    _____

    _____

    _____

    _____

(Item 2) CD1 Track 66

2. (i)   Where did the accident happen and how many were killed and injured?

_____

_____

(ii) Mention any **two** details about the people killed in the accident.

_____

_____

(Item 3) CD1 Track 67

3. What is hoped to be achieved for children in the context of International Children's Day? Mention any **three** details.

_____

_____

_____

(Item 4) CD1 Track 68

4. (i)   What caused the casualties in the Philippines?

_____

_____

(ii) What effects did the catastrophe have?

_____

_____

(Item 5) CD1 Track 69

5. Weather Forecast
    (i)   What has given rise to the current weather conditions?

_____

_____

(ii) What type of weather is expected today?

_____

_____

Wortschatz

der Alkohol – *alcohol*
der Alkoholkonsum – *the consumption of alcohol*
die Droge(-n) – *drug(s)*
drogenabhängig – *addicted to drugs*
das Rauschgift – *drugs*
der Drogenhändler(-) – *drug dealer(s)*
die Tablette(-n) – *tablet(s)*
die Sucht – *addiction*
der/die Süchtige – *addict*
der Gruppenzwang – *peer pressure*
süchtig – *addicted*
schmuggeln – *to smuggle*
inhalieren – *to inhale*
rauchen – *to smoke*
spritzen – *to inject*
Gesundheitsschäden – *damage to health*
das Selbstwertgefühl – *self-esteem*
die Kriminalität – *crime*
sterben – *to die*

Test 8

German – Higher Level
LISTENING COMPREHENSION

First Part

CD2 Track 2

The interview will be played **three** times: first right through, then in segments with pauses, and finally right through again.

1. What do you learn about Frau Steinhoff? Give **three** details.

_____

_____

_____

2. (i)   What age was Frau Steinhoff's daughter when she started taking drugs?

    _____

    (ii) What reasons does she give for not noticing?

    _____

    _____

    _____

3. What changes did Frau Steinhoff's sister notice in the daughter's behaviour?

    _____

    _____

    _____

4. (i)   What evidence finally convinced her of her daughter's use of drugs?

    _____

    _____

    (ii) What other indicators were there?

    _____

    _____

5. (i)   Does her daughter still take drugs? Give details.

    _____

    _____

    (ii) What plans does her daughter have for the future?

    _____

    _____

Second Part

CD2 Track 3

You will now hear a telephone conversation. The receptionist takes a message from the caller.

To allow you to answer **Question 1** (**the note**), the phonecall will be played **twice**, with a pause after each playing during which you should **fill in the box**. The phonecall will then be played for a third and final time to allow you to answer **Question 2** (the **language** of the phonecall).

1. Write out **in German** the note that the receptionist will leave.
   (**Key words, not full sentences**)
   The note should contain:
   - ■ name of caller.
   - ■ problem caller wishes to discuss.
   - ■ message regarding further contact.
   - ■ telephone number of caller.

Anruf für: _____

Anruf von: _____

Nachricht (stichwortartig):
Problem: _____

_____

Der Anrufer:
- ☐ möchte einen Termin in einer Stunde.
- ☐ wird in einer Stunde angerufen werden.
- ☐ erhält in einer Stunde Besuch von einem Beamten.
- ☐ ruft in einer Stunde zurück.

Kontaktnummer: _____

Now answer Question 2.

2. After listening to the phonecall for the third time, pick out **three** examples of the language (**expressions and phrases, not tone of voice**) used in the phonecall that show the caller's **willingness to help**.

_____

_____

_____

Third Part

CD2 Track 4

You will now hear a conversation between **two** people. The dialogue will be played **three** times, with a pause after each playing. Answer in English.

1. (i) The two people involved are engaged in:
   - (a) a debate.
   - (b) a voxpop interview.
   - (c) an argument.
   - (d) a chat.

   Indicate your choice by putting **a, b, c** or **d** in the box provided. ☐

(ii) Find **two** indications in the conversation to support your choice.

_____

_____

2. (i) Which adjective best describes the girl's attitude during the conversation?
   (a) opposed
   (b) in favour
   (c) indifferent
   (d) uninterested

   Indicate your choice by putting **a**, **b**, **c** or **d** in the box provided. ☐

   (ii) Write down **two** details from the conversation to support your choice.

   _____

   _____

3. (i) Why does the girl drink alcohol? Give **two** reasons.

   _____

   _____

   (ii) How does she think her parents would react to what she has to say?
   Give details.

   _____

   _____

   _____

Fourth Part

You will now hear **four** news items taken from the radio, followed by the weather forecast. The news will be played **three** times; the first time right through, then in five segments with pauses, and finally right through again.

(Item 1)   `CD2 Track 5`

1. With the legislation of cannabis for limited medical use in Germany, in what types of product will it be made available?

   _____

   _____

   _____

(Item 2)   CD2 Track 6

2. (i)   More and more young Germans smoke. What are the latest findings?

_____

_____

    (ii) What demands is the Minister for Health making?

_____

_____

(Item 3)   CD2 Track 7

3. (i)   What are the main findings of the study mentioned here? Give details.

_____

_____

_____

    (ii) Give details of those involved in the study.

_____

_____

_____

(Item 4)   CD2 Track 8

4. (i)   What did customs officials discover and where was the discovery made?

    What: _____

    Where: _____

    (ii) Give details of the arrests made in relation to the discovery.

_____

_____

(Item 5)   CD2 Track 9

5. Weather Forecast
    What type of weather is expected
    (i)   for today?

_____

_____

    (ii) for the coming week?

_____

_____

Revision 4

1. Prices
   List the **ten** prices mentioned on the CD.

   _____   _____

   _____   _____

   _____   _____

   _____   _____

   _____   _____

2. Catastrophes.
   Translate the **ten** catastrophes mentioned on the CD.

   _____   _____

   _____   _____

   _____   _____

   _____   _____

   _____   _____

3. Car accidents.
   Translate the words and sentences related to accidents that are mentioned on the CD.

   _____   _____

   _____   _____

   _____   _____

   _____   _____

   _____   _____

4. Environment.
   Translate the **ten** environmental topics mentioned on the CD.

   _____   _____

   _____   _____

   _____   _____

   _____   _____

   _____   _____

5. In the home.
   Translate the **ten** household items mentioned on the CD.

   _____   _____

   _____   _____

   _____   _____

   _____   _____

   _____   _____

Wortschatz

sich vertragen mit (+ Dat.) – *to get on with*
auskommen mit (+ Dat.) – *to get on with*
schimpfen mit – *to give out to*
die Hausarbeit – *housework*
behandeln – *to treat*
drohen(+ Dat.) – *to threaten*
verprügeln – *to beat*
die Kindesmisshandlung – *child abuse*
die Verwahrlosung – *neglect*
das Taschengeld – *pocket-money*
streng – *strict*
lässig – *easy going*
der Streit – *quarrel*
ünterstützen – *to support*
die Unterstützung – *support*
der Lärm – *noise*
sich zanken – *to quarrel*

Test 9

German – Higher Level
LISTENING COMPREHENSION

First Part

CD2 Track 12

The interview will be played **three** times: first right through, then in segments with pauses, and finally right through again.

1. (i)   Which section of the newspaper does Heike want to look at?

[handwritten answer] agar eat room. / teach / airt le Panracht ✓

    (ii) What objections does her father offer?

[handwritten answer] an costas s oerdh ní i· teach léi féin
ur gó di bills a roc agus i'n
áil cian ē

2. What does Heike's morning look like at present?

~~[illegible] sí an~~ téann sí go dtí an Stáisiún ~~[illegible]~~ traein ag [illegible] agus sí an bus. ✓ + Luas/tram.

3. What arguments does she use to persuade her father?

tá níos mó tam saor aici

Beidh sí go breá tá gardaí aici ann sa city agus is city girl í ~~[illegible]~~ they will go to [illegible]

4. (i) What details are we given about Silvia?

~~([illegible]) (tá sí ina cónaí leis)~~ ~~(colleague)~~ ó a [illegible] scoil – tá árasán aici sa cathair

(ii) Why might Heike be able to share with Silvia?

mar tá cónaí orthu leis. co workers.

5. (i) Why is Heike's father now in favour of Heike's proposal?

Beidh sí sábháilte. tá [illegible] fios aige Silvia

(ii) How does he propose helping Heike with her decision?

~~[illegible]~~ Beidh dinnéar acu le chéile next month. Tabharfaidh sé [illegible] [illegible] cion cúpla 6 mí

Second Part

CD2 Track 13

You will now hear a telephone conversation. The secretary of 'Action Concept' in Cologne takes a message.

To allow you to answer **Question 1** (**the note**), the phonecall will be played **twice,** with a pause after each playing during which you should **fill in the box.** The phonecall will then be played for a third and final time to allow you to answer **Question 2** (the **language** of the phonecall).

1. Write out **in German** the key information the secretary jots down as a memo to her boss on his return.

   (**Key words, not full sentences**)

   The note should contain:
   ■ the caller's name.
   ■ problem caller wishes to discuss.
   ■ details regarding further contact.
   ■ telephone number of caller.

   Anruf von: _Robin._

   Problem: _Id K_ ~~stop Ap~~

   _____

   Der Anrufer:
   ✓ ruft morgen zurück.
   ☐ schickt eine Email.
   ☐ wird morgen zurückgerufen.
   ☐ wird dem Direktor einen Brief schreiben.

   Kontaktnummer: _803 720_
   _8337420_   _83 74 20_

Now answer Question 2.

2. After listening to the phonecall for the third time, pick out **three** examples of the language (**expressions and phrases, not tone of voice**) used by the caller to express how worried he is.

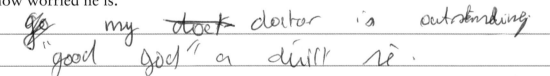

   go my ~~doct~~ doctor is outstanding
   "good god" a duill re.

   _____

Third Part

CD2 Track 14

You will now hear a conversation between **two** people. The dialogue will be played **three** times, with a pause after each playing. Answer in English.

1. (i) The conversation is between:
   (a) a boyfriend and girlfriend.
   (b) a brother and sister.
   (c) a mother and son.
   (d) a husband and wife.

   Indicate your choice by putting **a**, **b**, **c** or **d** in the box provided. | d |

(ii) Find **two** indications in the conversation to support your answer.

_____

_____

2. (i) Which adjective best describes the female's reaction for most of the conversation?
    (a) grateful
    (b) suspicious
    (c) angry
    (d) indifferent

    Indicate your choice by putting **a**, **b**, **c** or **d** in the box provided. ☐ c ✓

    (ii) Find **two** indications in the conversation to support your answer.

    Tá sí cromtha go bhfuil ann bille /fón £91

    Tá sé in iomarca

3. What decision does the female speaker come to at the end of the conversation? Give details.

    Tá cheann féin fón póca ááá eirge

    nó tá an bille ró chostasach

Fourth Part

You will now hear **four** news items taken from the radio, followed by the weather forecast. The news will be played **three** times; the first time right through, then in five segments with pauses, and finally right through again.

(Item 1)   CD2 Track 15
  1. (i) Why was the couple brought before the court?

      _____

      _____

    (ii) What excuse did the couple give for their action?

      _____

      _____

(Item 2)   CD2 Track 16
  2. What service does Schüler Notruf Center provide? Mention any **three** details.

      _____

      _____

      _____

(Item 3) CD2 Track 17

3. (i) What was the subject of the study mentioned here?

Staidéir ar pairstí agus tuintí

(ii) What were the main findings of the study? Mention any **two** details.

(Item 4) CD2 Track 18

4. (i) What proposal was made by the CSU General Secretary and what does he hope to achieve as a result?

(ii) What types of crime are typical for young culprits, according to the General Secretary?

(Item 5) CD2 Track 19

5. Weather Forecast
    (i) What is the weather forecast for today? Mention **three** details.

    (ii) What is the weather forecast for the next day?

Wortschatz

der Job – *part-time job*
arbeiten – *to work*
der Verdienst – *earnings*
verdienen – *to earn*
Guthaben – *credit*
das Handy(-s) – *mobile phone*
ausgehen – *to go out*
sich (Dat.) leisten – *to afford*
Regale auffüllen – *to stack shelves*
babysitten – *to babysit*
die Kasse – *(cash) till*
als Kellner/-in – *as a waiter/waitress*

Test 10

German – Higher Level

LISTENING COMPREHENSION

First Part

CD2 Track 22

The interview will be played **three** times: first right through, then in segments with pauses, and finally right through again.

1. Why is Anna fed up? Explain giving **two** details.

   _____

   _____

2. Thomas has found work.
   (i) How did he get the job?

   _____

   (ii) What does the job entail?

   _____

   _____

3. What details does Thomas give about pay and work times? Mention **three** details.

_____

_____

4. How long does a tour last and how many people are in a group?

_____

_____

5. Anna is interested in Thomas's work.
(i) What are the requirements for getting this kind of job?

_____

_____

_____

(ii) Apart from money, what are the other benefits of this kind of work? Mention any **two**.

_____

_____

Second Part

CD2 Track 23

You will now hear a telephone conversation. The receptionist takes a message from the caller.

To allow you to answer **Question 1 (the note)**, the phonecall will be played **twice**, with a pause after each playing during which you should **fill in the box**. The phonecall will then be played for a third and final time to allow you to answer **Question 2** (the **language** of the phonecall).

1. Write out **in German** the note which the receptionist will leave.
(**Key words, not full sentences**)
The note should contain:
- whom the caller wishes to speak to.
- name of caller.
- problem caller wishes to discuss.
- message regarding further contact.
- telephone number of caller.

Anruf für: _____

Anruf von: _____

Nachricht (stichwortartig):

Problem: _____

_____

Der Anrufer:

☐ ruft zurück.

☐ wartet auf Ihren Rückruf.

☐ kommt persönlich vorbei.

☐ möchte einen Termin.

Kontaktnummer: _____

Now answer Question 2.

2. After listening to the phonecall for the third time, pick out **three** examples of the language (**expressions and phrases, not tone of voice**) used by the caller to convince the receptionist of her difficulty.

_____

_____

_____

CD2 Track 24

Third Part

You will now hear a conversation between **two** people. The dialogue will be played **three** times, with a pause after each playing. Answer in English.

1. (i) The conversation is between:

   (a) a teacher and a pupil.

   (b) a father and daughter.

   (c) an employer and a pupil on work experience.

   (d) two colleagues at work.

   Indicate your choice by putting **a**, **b**, **c** or **d** in the box provided. ☐

   (ii) Find **two** indications in the conversation to support your choice.

   _____

   _____

2. (i) Which adjective best describes Frau Lorenz's attitude during the conversation?
   (a) indifferent
   (b) rude
   (c) embarrassed
   (d) enthusiastic

   Indicate your choice by putting **a**, **b**, **c** or **d** in the box provided.

   (ii) Give **two** reasons for your choice.

   _____

   _____

3. (i) As the conversation goes on, do you notice any change in the attitude of:
   (a) Herr Kramer
   (b) Frau Lorenz
   Explain your answer with reference to the conversation.

   _____

   _____

   (ii) What does Herr Kramer decide to do in the end?

   _____

   _____

Fourth Part

You will now hear **four** news items taken from the radio, followed by the weather forecast. The news will be played **three** times; the first time right through, then in five segments with pauses, and finally right through again.

(Item 1)   CD2 Track 25
1. Mention any **three** details of the Youth Protection Act (*Jugendschutzgesetz*).

   _____

   _____

   _____

(Item 2)   CD2 Track 26
2. (i) What is the minimum age for young people who wish to work part-time?
   In which areas are exceptions allowed?

   _____

   _____

(ii) Between which times are young people allowed to work? Mention **two** exceptions to these limits?

_____

_____

(Item 3)   CD2 Track 27

3. (i) According to the study, what percentage of students work during term-time?

_____

(ii) What proportion work during holiday time and for how long?

_____

_____

(Item 4)   CD2 Track 28

4. (i) What are school students in Hamburg planning to do on Day for Africa?

_____

_____

(ii) How many pupils are participating?

_____

(Item 5)   CD2 Track 29

5. Weather Forecast
What kind of weather is expected for:
(i) today?

_____

_____

_____

(ii) in the near future?

_____

_____

_____

Revision 5

CD4

1. List the **ten** numbers mentioned on the CD.

   _____   _____
   _____   _____
   _____   _____
   _____   _____
   _____   _____

2. Home.
   Translate the **ten** household words mentioned on the CD.

   _____   _____
   _____   _____
   _____   _____
   _____   _____
   _____   _____

3. Travel.
   Translate the **ten** travel items mentioned on the CD.

   _____   _____
   _____   _____
   _____   _____
   _____   _____
   _____   _____

4. Reading Materials.
   Translate the **ten** reading materials mentioned on the CD.

   _____   _____
   _____   _____
   _____   _____
   _____   _____
   _____   _____

5. Clothing.
   Translate the **ten** items of clothing mentioned on the CD.

   _____   _____
   _____   _____
   _____   _____
   _____   _____

mobben – *to bully*
Mobbing – *bullying*
einschüchtern – *to intimidate*
das Opfer(-) – *victim*
der/die Täter/in – *culprit*
die Gewalt – *violence*
ausgrenzen – *to isolate/exclude*
schlagen – *to hit*
anpöbeln – *to abuse (slang)*
beschimpfen – *to insult*
zusammenschlagen – *to beat up*
die Angst – *fear*
strafen – *to punish*
Streber(-) – *swot*
Schleimer(-) – *teacher's pet*
Geld erpressen – *to extort money*
leistungsstark – *good (performing)*
leistungsschwach – *weak (performing)*

Test 11

German – Higher Level

LISTENING COMPREHENSION

First Part

CD2 Track 32

The interview will be played **three** times: first right through, then in segments with pauses, and finally right through again.

1. What do we learn about Jan L. from the interviewer?

_____

_____

_____

2. (i) According to Dr Richter, what statistics show that bullying is a widespread problem?

_____

_____

_____

(ii) What advice does he give to those who feel threatened?

_____

_____

_____

3. (i) How should one react if one sees someone being beaten up in school?

_____

_____

_____

(ii) What should one do if one notices a fight about to begin?

_____

_____

_____

4. What should one say to those acting in an aggressive manner or consuming alcohol and other drugs?

_____

_____

_____

5. (i) In what ways does bullying by girls differ from that of boys?

_____

_____

_____

(ii) What concrete advice does Dr Richter give Jan L.'s parents?

_____

_____

_____

Second Part

CD2 Track 33

You will now hear a telephone conversation. Frau Meier takes a message from the caller.

To allow you to answer **Question 1 (the note)**, the phonecall will be played **twice**, with a pause after each playing during which you should **fill in the box**. The phonecall will then be played for a third and final time to allow you to answer **Question 2** (the **language** of the phonecall).

1. Write out **in German** the note which the Frau Meier will leave.
   (**Key words, not full sentences**)
   The note should contain:
   - whom the caller wishes to speak to.
   - name of caller.
   - problem caller wishes to discuss.
   - message regarding further contact.
   - telephone number of caller.

Anruf für: _____

Anruf von: _____

Nachricht (stichwortartig):
Problem: _____

_____

Der Anrufer:

☐ ruft wieder an.

☐ wartet auf Ihren Rückruf.

☐ hat zurückgerufen.

☐ möchte Sie treffen.

Telefonnummer: _____

Now answer Question 2.

2. After listening to the phonecall for the third time, pick out **three** examples of the language (**expressions and phrases, not tone of voice**) used in the phonecall to convey the **urgency** of the matter in question.

_____

_____

_____

Third Part

You will now hear a conversation between Angela and Ulf. The dialogue will be played **three** times, with a pause after each playing. Answer in English.

1. (i) The conversation is between:
    (a) boyfriend and girlfriend.
    (b) two neighbours.
    (c) two classmates.
    (d) brother and sister.

    Indicate your choice by putting **a**, **b**, **c** or **d** in the box provided.

    (ii) Find **two** indications in the conversation to support your choice.

    _____

    _____

2. (i) Which adjective best describes Ulf's state of mind during the conversation?
    (a) uneasy
    (b) amused
    (c) bored
    (d) tired

    Indicate your choice by putting **a**, **b**, **c** or **d** in the box provided.

    (ii) Write down **two** details from the conversation to support your choice.

    _____

    _____

3. (i) How does Angela interpret Ulf's situation? Give details.

    _____

    _____

    _____

    (ii) Angela comes up with a number of practical steps for Ulf to deal with the situation he is in. What are they?

    _____

    _____

    _____

Fourth Part

You will now hear **four** news items taken from the radio, followed by the weather forecast. The news will be played **three** times; the first time right through, then in five segments with pauses, and finally right through again.

(Item 1)   CD2 Track 35

1. (i)   Why was a girl in England sentenced to 18 months in prison? Give details.

_____

_____

(ii) Apart from a term in prison, what other punishment did she receive?

_____

_____

(Item 2)   CD2 Track 36

2. (i)   Give details of the study carried out by the University of Lindau.

_____

_____

(ii) How many pupils in Germany have been the victims of cyber-bullying?

_____

_____

(Item 3)   CD2 Track 37

3. (i)   What statistics does the EU quote to back up its claims about cyber-bullying?

_____

_____

(ii) Give **two** details about 'Safe Internet Day'.

_____

_____

(Item 4)   CD2 Track 38

4. Who started the anti-bullying initiative and what does he hope to achieve?

_____

_____

_____

_____

_____

(Item 5)

CD2 Track 39

5. Weather Forecast

    (i)   To which states does the weather forecast apply?

              _____

              _____

    (ii) What type of weather is forecast for today?

              _____

              _____

Wortschatz

kennen lernen – *to get to know*
besprechen – *to discuss*
diskutieren – *to discuss (general)*
die Eigenschaft(-en) – *quality*
der Freund(-e) – *male friend/boyfriend*
die Freundin(-innen) – *female friend/girlfriend*
lieben – *to love*
die Liebe – *love*
sich verlieben – *to fall in love*
Schluss machen mit (+Dat.) – *to break it off with*
miteinander gehen – *to go with one another*
sich treffen mit (+ Dat.) – *to meet (by arrangement)*
ablenken – *to distract*
erzählen – *to tell*

Test 12

German – Higher Level

LISTENING COMPREHENSION

First Part

CD2 Track 42

The interview will be played **three** times: first right through, then in segments with pauses, and finally right through again.

1. (i) Hannes works in a Children's Hospital. What does his job entail?

   _____

   _____

   (ii) Hannes explains how important his job is to sick children. Give **two** details.

   _____

   _____

2. Give details of Hannes' training. (Duration; name and location of training school; etc.)

    _____

    _____

    _____

    _____

3. (i)   What subjects are on the timetable for all students training for the profession?

          _____

          _____

          _____

          _____

    (ii) Part of the training is specifically geared to dealing with sick children.
          What does this element of training cover?

          _____

          _____

          _____

          _____

4. How does Hannes prepare for his job in the morning? Give **four** details.

    _____

    _____

    _____

    _____

5. Hannes visited two children that morning. What did he do in each case that cheered
    them up?

    _____

    _____

    _____

    _____

Second Part

CD2 Track 43

You will now hear a telephone conversation. Peter has to pass on a message from the caller to a friend of his.

To allow you to answer **Question 1** (**the note**), the phonecall will be played **twice**, with a pause after each playing during which you should **fill in the box**. The phonecall will then be played for a third and final time to allow you to answer **Question 2** (the **language** of the phonecall).

1. Write out **in German** the note which Peter jots down.
   (**Key words, not full sentences**)
   The note should contain:
   - to whom the caller wishes to pass on a message.
   - name of caller.
   - problem caller wishes to discuss.
   - message regarding further contact (how, when).
   - telephone number of caller.

Anruf für: _____

Anruf von: _____

Nachricht (stichwortartig):
Problem: _____

_____

Der Anrufer:
- [ ]   ruft zurück.
- [ ]   wartet auf Rückruf.
- [ ]   kommt persönlich vorbei.
- [ ]   möchte ein Treffen.

Telefonnummer des Anrufers: _____

Now answer Question 2.
2. After listening to the phonecall for the third time, pick out **three** examples of the language (**expressions and phrases, not tone of voice**) used by the caller that show her **joy**.

_____

_____

_____

Third Part

CD2 Track 44

You will now hear a conversation between two people. The dialogue will be played **three** times, with a pause after each playing. Answer in English.

1. (i)   The conversation is between:
     (a) a father and daughter.
     (b) a schoolgirl and her brother.
     (c) a girlfriend and boyfriend.
     (d) a girl and her cousin.

     Indicate your choice by putting **a, b, c** or **d** in the box provided.

   (ii)   Find **two** indications in the conversation to support your choice.

   _____

   _____

2. (i)   Which adjective best describes Marie's attitude during the conversation?
     (a) indifferent
     (b) enthusiastic
     (c) worried
     (d) angry

     Indicate your choice by putting **a, b, c** or **d** in the box provided.

   (ii)   Give **two** details from the conversation to support your choice.

   _____

   _____

   (iii) What does Dirk want to do when he finishes Tenth Class?

   _____

   _____

3. Why does Marie seem to be relieved at the end of the conversation?

   _____

   _____

   _____

   _____

Fourth Part

You will now hear **four** news items taken from the radio, followed by the weather forecast. The news will be played **three** times; the first time right through, then in five segments with pauses, and finally right through again.

(Item 1)   CD2 Track 45
  1. (i) What special offer is available from the marketing company?

_____

_____

     (ii) What is Facebook against?

_____

_____

(Item 2)   CD2 Track 46
  2. (i) From which countries do the young people come?

_____

_____

     (ii) What are the young people asked to do? Give details.

_____

_____

(Item 3)   CD2 Track 47
  3. (i) What is the main finding issued by the scientists?

_____

_____

     (ii) In which cases are friendships particularly important?

_____

_____

(Item 4)   CD2 Track 48
  4. (i) What do the Polish and German governments regard as a political necessity?

_____

_____

     (ii) Which particular matter could cause problems between the two countries?

_____

_____

(Item 5)

CD2 Track 49

5. Weather Forecast

   (i)   What has caused the change in the weather? Give details.

_____

_____

_____

   (ii)   What type of weather is forecast for today?

_____

_____

_____

Revision 6

1. Weights and measures.
   List the **five** measures and **five** weights mentioned on the CD.

   _____   _____
   _____   _____
   _____   _____
   _____   _____
   _____   _____

2. Part-time jobs.
   Translate the **ten** part-time jobs mentioned on the CD.

   _____   _____
   _____   _____
   _____   _____
   _____   _____
   _____   _____

3. Work.
   Translate the **ten** work-related vocabulary items mentioned on the CD.

   _____   _____
   _____   _____
   _____   _____
   _____   _____
   _____   _____

4. Industries.
   Translate the **ten** industries mentioned on the CD.

   _____   _____
   _____   _____
   _____   _____
   _____   _____
   _____   _____

5. Means of transport.
   Translate the **ten** means of transport mentioned on the CD.

   _____   _____
   _____   _____
   _____   _____
   _____   _____
   _____   _____

Wortschatz

der Deutsche/die Deutsche – *German man/woman*
die Deutschen – *the Germans*
Menschen deutscher Abstammung – *people of German origin*
lässig – *casual/easy-going*
das Bundesland (-länder) – *Federal state*
der Bundeskanzler/die Bundeskanzlerin – *Federal Chancellor (= Taoiseach)*
der Bundestag – *parliament (= Dáil)*
der/die Bundestagsabgeordnete – *Member of Parliament (= TD)*
die Insel(n) – *island(s)*
die Bevölkerung – *population*
das Essen – *food*
das Wetter – *weather*
das Klima – *climate*
die Kriminalität – *crime*
sportlich – *into sport*
musikalisch – *musical*
der Sinn für Humor – *sense of humour*
das Klischee(-s) – *cliché*
die Konjunktur – *economy/economic activity*
das Wirtschaftswunder – *economic miracle*
der Gastarbeiter(-) – *guest worker (immigrant worker)*
die Berliner Mauer – *the Berlin Wall*
die Teilung deutschlands – *partition of Germany*
die Wiedervereinigung – *reunification*
der Erste/der Zweite Weltkrieg – *the First/Second World War*
das Dritte Reich – *the Third Reich*

Test 13

German – Higher Level
LISTENING COMPREHENSION

First Part

CD2 Track 52

The interview will be played **three** times: first right through, then in segments with pauses, and finally right through again.

1. (i) What does Herr Saris work at?

    _____

    (ii) How many work in the firm in total and how many foreigners work there?

    _____

    _____

2. (i) How many hours does he work per week?

    _____

    (ii) Does he do overtime work? Explain why/why not.

    _____

    _____

3. In earlier years, Herr Saris helped out in the personnel section.
    (i) Who came to him for help?

    _____

    _____

    (ii) What problems had they, and why?

    _____

    _____

4. Mention **three** things he says about the Germans.

    _____

    _____

    _____

5. (i) Mention **two** negative aspects about living in Germany.

    _____

    _____

    (ii) What do Herr Saris and his wife plan to do in a few years time?

    _____

    _____

    _____

Second Part

You will now hear a telephone conversation. The receptionist takes a message from the caller.

To allow you to answer **Question 1** (**the note**), the phonecall will be played **twice**, with a pause after each playing during which you should **fill in the box**. The phonecall will then be played for a third and final time to allow you to answer **Question 2** (the **language** of the phonecall).

1. Write out **in German** the note which the receptionist will leave.
    (**Key words, not full sentences**)
    The note should contain:
    - to whom the caller wishes to pass on a message.
    - name of caller.
    - problem caller wishes to discuss.
    - message regarding further contact (how, when).
    - telephone number of caller.

Anruf für: _____

Anruf von: _____

Nachricht (stichwortartig):

Problem: _____

_____

Der Anrufer:
☐ ruft zurück.
☐ wartet auf Rückruf.
☐ erbittet Email.
☐ möchte einen Termin.

Telefonnummer des Anrufers: _____

Now answer Question 2.
2. After listening to the phonecall for the third time, pick out **three** examples of the language (**expressions and phrases, not tone of voice**) used by the caller that show his **annoyance**.

_____

_____

Third Part

CD2 Track 54

You will now hear a conversation between two people. The dialogue will be played **three** times, with a pause after each playing.

1. (i) The conversation is between:
      (a) two unemployed people.
      (b) a husband and wife.
      (c) a boss and an employee.
      (d) a child-minder and the father of the child.

   Indicate your choice by putting **a**, **b**, **c** or **d** in the box provided. ☐

   (ii) Find **two** indications in the conversation to support your choice.

   _____

   _____

2. (i) Which adjective best describes Regina's attitude during the conversation?
      (a) delighted
      (b) shocked
      (c) uninterested
      (d) disappointed

   Indicate your choice by putting **a**, **b**, **c** or **d** in the box provided. ☐

   (ii) Give **two** details from the conversation to support your choice.

   _____

   _____

3. (i) What excuse does Werner give Regina for not contacting her? Give details.

   _____

   _____

   _____

   _____

   (ii) What good news has Werner for Regina at the end of the conversation? Give details.

   _____

   _____

   _____

   _____

Fourth Part

You will now hear **four** news items taken from the radio, followed by the weather forecast. The news will be played **three** times; the first time right through, then in five segments with pauses, and finally right through again.

(Item 1)   `CD2 Track 55`

1. (i)   In what year is this great world fair to take place, and where?

_____

_____

    (ii)   How many visitors are expected to come there each day?

_____

(Item 2)   `CD2 Track 56`

2.   Increase in the number of women employed by federal bodies.
    (i)   How great was the increase?

_____

_____

    (ii)   How many women were in public employment in June?

_____

(Item 3)   `CD2 Track 57`

3. (i)   The Egmont publishing company carried out a recent study in Germany. Mention **two** details about the study.

_____

_____

    (ii)   Mention **two** priority items on the shopping list of the people who were surveyed.

_____

_____

(Item 4)   `CD2 Track 58`

4. (i)   How many people in Germany are estimated to be infected with AIDS?

_____

    (ii)   What service is being provided by the Neuss Health Board?

_____

_____

_____

(Item 5)

CD2 Track 59

5. Weather Forecast

   (i)   What type of weather is forecast for Monday?

   _____

   _____

   (ii) What is the outlook for the next few days?

   _____

   _____

Wortschatz

obdachlos – *homeless*
die Obdachlosigkeit – *homelessness*
der/die Obdachlose(-n) – *the homeless person(s)*
das Mitleid – *sympathy*
das Obdachlosenasyl – *homeless shelter*
der Penner – *tramp*
das Straßenkind(-er) – *street child*
der Ausreißer – *runaway*
ausreißen – *to run away (from home)*
der Türeingang – *doorway*
die Bank – *bench*
betteln – *to beg*
die Almosen – *alms*
Essen auf Rädern – *Meals on Wheels*
die karitative Organisation – *charitable organisation*
erfrieren – *to freeze to death*
der Alkoholiker(-) – *alcoholic*
der/die Süchtige – *addict*
sich kümmern um (+Akk.) – *to look after/care for*

Test 14

German – Higher Level

LISTENING COMPREHENSION

First Part

CD2 Track 62

The interview will be played **three** times: first right through, then in segments with pauses, and finally right through again.

1. (i) Where is the hostel situated?

_____

(ii) Who does the hostel cater for?

_____

_____

2. (i) What services does the hostel provide for those who come there?

_____

_____

_____

(ii) What **two** conditions do the visitors have to fulfil if they wish to stay longer?

_____

_____

3. (i) Describe the room, mentioning **three** details.

_____

_____

_____

(ii) Why do young people come to the hostel?

_____

_____

_____

4. What information are we given about Florian? Mention any **four** details.

_____

_____

_____

_____

5. How do the visitors to the hostel spend their evenings after their meal?

_____

_____

_____

_____

_____

Second Part

You will now hear a telephone conversation. The volunteer takes a message from the caller.

To allow you to answer **Question 1** (**the note**), the phonecall will be played **twice**, with a pause after each playing during which you should **fill in the box**. The phonecall will then be played for a third and final time to allow you to answer **Question 2** (the **language** of the phonecall).

1. Write out **in German** the note which the volunteer will leave.
    (**Key words, not full sentences**)
    The note should contain:
    - ■ to whom the caller wishes to pass on a message.
    - ■ name of caller.
    - ■ problem caller wishes to discuss.
    - ■ message regarding further contact (how, when).
    - ■ telephone number of caller.

Anruf für: _____

Anruf von: _____

Nachricht (stichwortartig):
Problem: _____

_____

Der Anrufer:
- ☐ ruft zurück.
- ☐ wartet auf Rückruf.
- ☐ sucht einen Platz.
- ☐ möchte einen Termin.

Telefonnummer des Anrufers: _____

Now answer Question 2.
2. After listening to the phonecall for the third time, pick out **three** examples of the language (**expressions and phrases, not tone of voice**) used by the caller that show her **dissatisfaction**.

_____

_____

_____

Third Part

CD2 Track 64

You will now hear a conversation between two people. The dialogue will be played **three** times, with a pause after each playing.

1. (i) The two people talking are:

   (a) two homeless people.
   (b) a homeless person and a teacher.
   (c) a teacher and a past pupil.
   (d) two voluntary workers.

   Indicate your choice by putting **a**, **b**, **c** or **d** in the box provided. ☐

   (ii) Find **two** indications in the conversation which support your choice.

   _____

   _____

2. (i) Which adjective best describes Bastian's attitude during the conversation?

   (a) delighted
   (b) committed
   (c) uninterested
   (d) disappointed

   Indicate your choice by putting **a**, **b**, **c** or **d** in the box provided. ☐

   (ii) Give **two** details from the conversation to support your choice.

   _____

   _____

3. (i) What exactly is Bastian doing when he meets Frau Keitmann? Give details.

   _____

   _____

   _____

   (ii) What suggestion does Frau Keitmann make to Bastian at the end of the conversation?

   _____

   _____

   _____

Fourth Part

You will now hear **four** news items taken from the radio, followed by the weather forecast. The news will be played **three** times; the first time right through, then in five segments with pauses, and finally right through again.

(Item 1)   CD2 Track 65

1. (i)   What has the survey in Hamburg revealed? Give details.

_____

_____

_____

   (ii)   How many people in Hamburg state that they are living rough?

_____

_____

_____

(Item 2)   CD2 Track 66

2. (i)   By how much have donations to Verein CaFee gone down and to what do they attribute this?

_____

_____

   (ii)   What effect has this had on their work? Give details.

_____

_____

(Item 3)   CD2 Track 67

3. (i)   According to this news item, what are the consequences of the floods in West Africa?

_____

_____

_____

   (ii)   What are the biggest problems in Senegal and Burkina Faso?

_____

_____

_____

(Item 4) CD2 Track 68

4. (i) What demand has been made by Caritas? Give details.

_____

_____

_____

(ii) Where in particular are more facilities needed?

_____

_____

_____

(Item 5) CD2 Track 69

5. Weather Forecast

(i) To which parts of Germany does the forecast apply?

_____

_____

_____

(ii) What is the weather forecast (a) for the rest of the day and (b) for tomorrow?

_____

_____

_____

Revision 7

1. Percentages.
   List the **ten** percentages mentioned on the CD.

   _____   _____

   _____   _____

   _____   _____

   _____   _____

   _____   _____

2. Work.
   Translate the **ten** work-related vocabulary items mentioned on the CD.

   _____   _____

   _____   _____

   _____   _____

   _____   _____

   _____   _____

3. School.
   Translate the **ten** school-related words mentioned on the CD.

   _____   _____

   _____   _____

   _____   _____

   _____   _____

   _____   _____

4. Eating and drinking.
   Translate the **ten** food and drink items mentioned on the CD.

   _____   _____

   _____   _____

   _____   _____

   _____   _____

   _____   _____

5. Feelings and emotions.
   Translate the **ten** feelings and emotions mentioned on the CD.

   _____   _____

   _____   _____

   _____   _____

   _____   _____

Wortschatz

die Rücksicht – *consideration*
anpöbeln – *to insult/abuse (slang)*
(un)höflich – *(im)polite*
Rücksicht nehmen auf (+ Akk.) – *to have consideration for*
Respekt zeigen – *to show respect*
die Respektlosigkeit – *disrespect*
der Wert(e) – *value(s)*
(un)freundlich – *friendly*
ignorieren – *to ignore*
die Ellenbogengesellschaft – *elbow society*
Manieren – *manners*
das Benehmen – *behaviour*
beleidigen – *to insult*
der Lärm – *noise*
diskriminieren – *to discriminate*
auslachen – *to make fun of, laugh at*
die Zivilcourage – *courage of one's convictions*
die (In-)Toleranz – *(in-)tolerance*

Test 15

German – Higher Level

LISTENING COMPREHENSION

First Part

CD3 Track 2

The interview will be played **three** times: first right through, then in segments with pauses, and finally right through again.

1. (i)   Where is Stefan working?

    _____

    _____

    (ii)   How long has he been working there?

    _____

2. (i) Mention any **three** institutions in which this type of social service (*Zivildienst*) is possible.

_____

_____

_____

(ii) How long does the social service last?

_____

_____

3. Describe what Stefan has to do as part of the morning shift.

_____

_____

_____

_____

_____

_____

4. What does he particularly like about the work he is doing at present?

_____

_____

_____

_____

_____

5. What reasons does Stefan give for not wanting to do military service? Give details.

_____

_____

_____

_____

_____

_____

Second Part

You will now hear a telephone conversation. The receptionist takes a message from the caller.

To allow you to answer **Question 1** (**the note**), the phonecall will be played **twice**, with a pause after each playing during which you should **fill in the box**. The phonecall will then be played for a third and final time to allow you to answer **Question 2** (the **language** of the phonecall).

1. Write out **in German** the note which the receptionist will leave.
   (**Key words, not full sentences**)
   The note should contain:
   - ◼ to whom the caller wishes to pass on a message.
   - ◼ name of caller.
   - ◼ problem caller wishes to discuss.
   - ◼ message regarding further contact (how, when).
   - ◼ telephone number of caller.

Anruf für: _____

Anruf von: _____

Nachricht (stichwortartig):
Problem: _____

_____

Der Anrufer:
- ☐ ruft zurück.
- ☐ wartet auf Rückruf.
- ☐ erbittet Email.
- ☐ möchte einen Termin.

Telefonnummer des Anrufers: _____

Now answer Question 2.
2. After listening to the phonecall for the third time, pick out **three** examples of the language (**expressions and phrases, not tone of voice**) used by the caller that show **anxiety**.

_____

_____

_____

Third Part

CD3 Track 4

You will now hear a conversation between two people. The dialogue will be played **three** times, with a pause after each playing.

1. The conversation is between:
   - (a) two parents.
   - (b) a principal and a teacher.
   - (c) a principal and a caretaker.
   - (d) an Art teacher and a P.E. teacher.

   Indicate your choice by putting **a**, **b**, **c** or **d** in the box provided. ▢

2. (i) Which adjective best describes Herr Hansen's attitude during the conversation?
   - (a) indifferent
   - (b) diplomatic
   - (c) annoyed
   - (d) helpful

   Indicate your choice by putting **a**, **b**, **c** or **d** in the box provided. ▢

   (ii) Write down **two** details from the conversation to support your choice.

   _____

   _____

3. (i) Frau Vogt treats Herr Hansen with great respect. Give **two** details that indicate this.

   _____

   _____

   (ii) What solution does Frau Vogt suggest to the problem Herr Hansen has identified?

   _____

   _____

   _____

   _____

   _____

   _____

   _____

Fourth Part

You will now hear **four** news items taken from the radio, followed by the weather forecast. The news will be played **three** times; the first time right through, then in five segments with pauses, and finally right through again.

(Item 1)   `CD3 Track 5`

1. (i) What areas must the police keep a close watch on, and why?

_____

_____

(ii) According to the police, what reasons are given for this misbehaviour?

_____

_____

(Item 2)   `CD3 Track 6`

2. (i) What is the theme of the new competition?

_____

(ii) What form can the competition entries take? Mention **three** forms.

_____

_____

_____

(Item 3)   `CD3 Track 7`

3. How many people were killed and how many were injured in the bank raid?

_____

_____

(Item 4)   `CD3 Track 8`

4. (i) When and where did the attacks by the right-wing extremists take place?

When: _____

Where: _____

(ii) What form did the main attack take? Mention **four** details.

_____

_____

_____

_____

(Item 5)

CD3 Track 9

5. Weather Forecast

(i) What kind of weather is forecast for today? Mention **two** details.

_____

_____

_____

(ii) What kind of weather is forecast for the next day?

_____

_____

_____

Wortschatz

besuchen – *to attend/to visit*
bestehen – *to pass*
durchfallen – *to fail*
das Fach (Fächer) – *subject(s)*
das Pflichtfach – *compulsory subject*
das Wahlfach – *optional subject*
die Arbeit(-en) – *test(s)*
die Note(n) – *grade(s)*
das Abitur – *Leaving Certificate*
die Schulordnung – *school rules*
die Schulpflicht – *compulsory schooling*
die Prüfung – *examination*
das Zeugnis(-se) – *school report*
die Zensur(-en) – *grade*
der Lehrplan – *syllabus*
sitzenbleiben – *to stay back*
pauken – *to swot/to work hard*
büffeln – *to swot/to work hard*

Test 16

German – Higher Level

LISTENING COMPREHENSION

First Part

CD3 Track 12

The interview will be played **three** times: first right through, then in segments with pauses, and finally right through again.

1. (i) How many pupils in total attend the Heinrich-Heyne-Gymnasium?

   _____

   (ii) Name the town and Federal State in which this school is situated.

   _____

   _____

2. School for the 180 'sports pupils' and for all other pupils is the same in many ways. Mention **three** of these similarities.

_____

_____

_____

3. (i) 'Sports pupils' at the Heinrich-Heyne-Gymnasium may engage in many types of sport. Mention any **three** of these.

_____

_____

_____

   (ii) When and how often do they train?

_____

_____

_____

_____

4. What, according to Herr Weber, is the key to the success of the school?

_____

_____

_____

_____

_____

5. It is expensive to run this school. Where does the money to run it come from?

_____

_____

_____

_____

_____

Second Part

CD3 Track 13

You will now hear a telephone conversation. The secretary takes a message from the caller.

To allow you to answer **Question 1** (**the note**), the phonecall will be played **twice**, with a pause after each playing during which you should **fill in the box**. The phonecall will then be played for a third and final time to allow you to answer **Question 2** (the **language** of the phonecall).

1. Write out **in German** the note which the secretary will leave.
    (**Key words, not full sentences**)
    The note should contain:
    ■ to whom the caller wishes to pass on a message.
    ■ name of caller.
    ■ problem caller wishes to discuss.
    ■ message regarding further contact/action to be taken.
    ■ telephone number of caller.

Anruf für: _____

Anruf von: _____

Nachricht (stichwortartig):
Problem: _____

_____

Der Anrufer:
☐ ruft später zurück.
☐ wird zu rückgerufen.
☐ kommt persönlich vorbei.
☐ möchte einen Termin.

Telefonnummer des Anrufers: _____

Now answer Question 2.

2. After listening to the phonecall for the third time, pick out **three** examples of the language (**expressions and phrases, not tone of voice**) used by the caller to express his **anger**.

_____

_____

_____

Third Part

CD3 Track 14

You will now hear a conversation between two people. The dialogue will be played **three** times, with a pause after each playing.

1. The conversation is between:
    (a) a mother and daughter.
    (b) two school friends.
    (c) twin sisters.
    (d) first cousins.

    Indicate your choice by putting **a**, **b**, **c** or **d** in the box provided.

2. (i) Which adjective best describes Stephanie's reactions to Martina's suggestion during the course of the conversation?
    (a) indifferent
    (b) doubtful
    (c) disappointed
    (d) enthusiastic

    Indicate your choice by putting **a**, **b**, **c** or **d** in the box provided.

    (ii) Write down **two** details from the conversation to support your choice.

    _____

    _____

3. (i) Why does Stephanie not agree to Martina's plan?

    _____

    _____

    _____

    _____

    _____

    (ii) What idea does Stephanie come up with for the following week?

    _____

    _____

    _____

    _____

    _____

Fourth Part

You will now hear **four** news items taken from the radio, followed by the weather forecast. The news will be played **three** times; the first time right through, then in five segments with pauses, and finally right through again.

(Item 1)   `CD3 Track 15`

1. (i) What were the main findings of the study into the school types chosen by German students? Mention any **two**.

_____

_____

    (ii) What percentage of students opt for a school (i) **below** and (ii) **above** their level of achievement?

_____

_____

(Item 2)   `CD3 Track 16`

2. (i) In what public places in Bremen will smoking be prohibited?

_____

    (ii) How many 17 to 18-year-old pupils smoke, according to the spokesman?

_____

(Item 3)   `CD3 Track 17`

3. Traffic news.
    (i) What is the cause of the chaotic conditions on the roads?

_____

    (ii) Where are the worst traffic-jams?

_____

(Item 4)   `CD3 Track 18`

4. (i) What have researchers discovered in relation to early school beginners? Mention any **two** details.

_____

_____

    (ii) According to researchers, what do teachers tend to not consider in relation to these children?

_____

(Item 5)   `CD3 Track 19`

5. Weather Forecast
    What type of weather is forecast:
    (i) for today?

_____

    (ii) for tomorrow?

_____

Revision 8

1. Numbers.
   Translate the **ten** number phrases mentioned on the CD.

   _____   _____

   _____   _____

   _____   _____

   _____   _____

   _____   _____

2. Titles.
   Translate the **ten** titles mentioned on the CD.

   _____   _____

   _____   _____

   _____   _____

   _____   _____

   _____   _____

3. German cities.
   List the names of the **ten** German cities mentioned on the CD.

   _____   _____

   _____   _____

   _____   _____

   _____   _____

   _____   _____

4. At the Lost and Found.
   Translate the **ten** items mentioned on the CD.

   _____   _____

   _____   _____

   _____   _____

   _____   _____

   _____   _____

5. Write down the **ten** words spelled out on the CD.

   _____   _____

   _____   _____

   _____   _____

   _____   _____

Sprachenlernen

Einheit 17

Wortschatz

die Sprache(-n) – *language(s)*
die Fremdsprache(-n) – *foreign language*
die Muttersprache(-n) – *native language*
die Alltagssprache – *everyday language*
die Umgangssprache – *colloquial language*
die Aussprache – *pronunciation*
die Grammatik – *grammar*
sprachbegabt – *having a talent for languages*
die Redewendung(-en) – *idiom(s)/phrase(s)*
fließend – *fluent(ly)*
die Sprache beherrschen – *to master the language*
die Betonung – *stress*
der Kurs(-e) – *course*
unterrichten – *to teach*
der Lehrer(-) – *(male) teacher*
die Lehrerin(-nen) – *(female) teacher*
die Vokabel(-n) – *word/vocabulary item*

Test 17

German – Higher Level

LISTENING COMPREHENSION

First Part

CD3 Track 22

The interview will be played **three** times: first right through, then in segments with pauses, and finally right through again.

1. (i)   Susi is not particularly happy with her studies at present. Give **two** reasons why?

She is stressed, it's difficult

(ii)   What is she tempted to do at this stage?

do a ff diff class that has
a friendly atmosphere

2. Mention **two** reasons why Susi prefers her second subject.

bc2 shis fluent , more range

3. (i) Name the **two** jobs Susi considers herself capable of doing. _secretry an office_

- Studio + shop a year in spanish School.

(ii) Mention **one** thing in particular that Susi can bring to each of these jobs.

goal M at french, a german teacher

4. (i) What does Günther suggest Susi should do?

_Do_

(ii) What **two** requirements have to be met to do what he suggests?

4 Simmestern

5. (i) Where can Susi get the application forms?

the Secratery

(ii) By what date must applications be in?

M november
_30_

Second Part

You will now hear a telephone conversation. The receptionist takes a message from the caller.

To allow you to answer **Question 1** (**the note**), the phonecall will be played **twice**, with a pause after each playing during which you should **fill in the box**. The phonecall will then be played for a third and final time to allow you to answer **Question 2** (the **language** of the phonecall).

1. Write out **in German** the note which the receptionist will leave.
    (**Key words, not full sentences**)
    The note should contain:
    - to whom the caller wishes to pass on a message.
    - name of caller.
    - problem caller wishes to discuss.
    - message regarding further contact.
    - telephone number of caller.

Anruf für: _Lemann_

Anruf von: _~~Str not kere~~ Karl, leamann_

Nachricht (stichwortartig):
Problem: _~~Kah Bektram~~ money, not learn_
french, note in french

Der Anrufer:
- [ ] ruft heute Nachmittag zurück.
- [ ] wartet auf eine SMS.
- [×] erbittet Ihren Rückruf.
- [ ] möchte einen Termin.

Telefonnummer des Anrufers: _~~Delkohm~~_
_05 04   37208608_

Now answer Question 2.

2. After listening to the phonecall for the third time, pick out **three** examples of the language (**expressions and phrases, not tone of voice**) used by the caller that show the caller's **dissatisfaction**.

    ich wille die per
    Das Kommen
    nicht gelernt
    wont lern french in uni

Third Part

You will now hear a conversation between two people. The dialogue will be played **three** times, with a pause after each playing.

1. The conversation is between:
   - (a) two teachers.
   - (b) a teacher and a pupil.
   - (c) two pupils.
   - (d) a student and an employer.

   Indicate your choice by putting **a, b, c** or **d** in the box provided.

2. (i) Which adjective best describes Anna's attitude during the first half of the conversation?
   - (a) indifferent
   - (b) diplomatic
   - (c) annoyed
   - (d) unhappy

   Indicate your choice by putting **a, b, c** or **d** in the box provided.

   (ii) Write down **two** details from the conversation to support your choice.

   _____

   _____

3. (i) What information does Anna wish to find out? Give details.

   _____

   _____

   _____

   _____

   _____

   (ii) What action does Karl suggest to help Anna? Give details.

   _____

   _____

   _____

   _____

   _____

Fourth Part

You will now hear **four** news items taken from the radio, followed by the weather forecast. The news will be played **three** times; the first time right through, then in five segments with pauses, and finally right through again.

(Item 1)   CD3 Track 25

1. (i) Against whom does the FPD chairman want sanctions introduced?

_____

_____

(ii) How does he justify his demand?

_____

_____

(Item 2)   CD3 Track 26

2. (i) What has been criticised by the chairman of the Teachers' Association?

_____

_____

(ii) According to the chairman, what are the reasons for the failings of primary schools?

_____

_____

_____

(Item 3)   CD3 Track 27

3. (i) Give details of the *Fremdsprachen* competition.

_____

_____

_____

(ii) According to the Minister of Education, what are the benefits of foreign languages?

_____

_____

_____

(Item 4)
CD3 Track 28

4. (i) What are the aims of the Network Project?

_____

_____

_____

   (ii) Give details of the Network Project.

_____

_____

_____

(Item 5)
CD3 Track 29

5. Weather Forecast
   (i) What kind of weather is forecast for today? Mention **three** details.

_____

_____

_____

   (ii) What kind of weather is expected in mountainous regions tomorrow? Mention **two** details.

_____

_____

Wortschatz

die Umwelt – *environment*
umweltbewusst – *environmentally aware*
zerstören – *to destroy*
der Umweltschutz – *environmental protection*
die Luft – *air*
die Verschmutzung – *pollution*
die globale Erwärmung – *global warming*
der steigende Meeresspiegel – *rising sea level*
der Gletscher(-) – *glacier*
schmelzen – *to melt*
das Kohlendioxid – *carbon dioxide*
der Müll – *rubbish*
sortieren – *to sort*
recyceln – *to recycle*
verbieten – *to ban*
die Tierart(-en) – *animal species*
der Lebensraum(-räume) – *habitat(s)*
aussterben – *to die out/to become extinct*
die Zukunft – *future*
die Solarenergie – *solar energy*
die Windenergie – *wind energy*

Test 18

German – Higher Level

LISTENING COMPREHENSION

First Part

CD3 Track 32

The interview will be played **three** times: first right through, then in segments with pauses, and finally right through again.

1. (i) Jens introduces himself at the beginning of the interview. Give **three** details about him.

   _____

   _____

   _____

   (ii) What is the aim of the group to which he belongs?

   _____

2. (i) Why did Jens and the other members think that there was a need for this group? Mention **four** details.

   _____

   _____

   _____

   _____

   (ii) What is their target in the first year?

   _____

   _____

3. What explanation does Jens give for the large amount of packaging in the rubbish bins? Give **two** details.

   _____

   _____

4. (i) Apart from packaging, what other concerns do Jens and his group have?

   _____

   _____

   (ii) Mention **two** statistical findings that Jens quotes to support his concerns.

   _____

   _____

5. (i) Mention **two** measures that Jens and his group intend introducing to achieve their targets.

   _____

   _____

   (ii) Jens and his group have already had some success. Mention **two** details.

   _____

   _____

Second Part

CD3 Track 33

You will now hear a telephone conversation. The official takes a message from the caller.

To allow you to answer **Question 1** (the note), the phonecall will be played **twice**, with a pause after each playing during which you should **fill in the box**. The phonecall will then be played for a third and final time to allow you to answer **Question 2** (the **language** of the phonecall).

1. Write out **in German** the note which the official will leave for his colleague.
   (**Key words, not full sentences**)
   The note should contain:
   - name of caller.
   - problem caller wishes to discuss.
   - message regarding further contact (how, when).
   - telephone number of caller.

Anruf von: _____

Nachricht (stichwortartig):
Problem: _____

_____

Der Anrufer:
- [ ] ruft zurück.
- [ ] wartet auf Rückruf.
- [ ] kommt morgen vorbei.
- [ ] möchte nicht angerufen werden.

Telefonnummer des Anrufers: _____

Now answer Question 2.
2. After listening to the phonecall for the third time, pick out **three** examples of the language (**expressions and phrases, not tone of voice**) used by the caller that show her **annoyance**.

_____

_____

_____

Third Part

CD3 Track 34

You will now hear a conversation between Lars and Frau Bergmann. The dialogue will be played **three** times, with a pause after each playing. Answer in English.

1. (i) The conversation is between:
   (a) old lady and stranger.
   (b) grandmother and nephew.
   (c) two neighbours.
   (d) two joggers in a park.

   Indicate your choice by putting **a, b, c** or **d** in the box provided. ☐

   (ii) Find **two** indications in the conversation to support your choice.

   _____

   _____

2. (i) Which adjective best describes Frau Bergmann's reaction during the conversation?
   (a) understanding
   (b) diplomatic
   (c) indifferent
   (d) annoyed

   Indicate your choice by putting **a, b, c** or **d** in the box provided. ☐

   (ii) Write down **two** details from the conversation to support your choice.

   _____

   _____

3. (i) Lars stands up for himself. Describe **two** of his arguments.

   _____

   _____

   (ii) What actions are Frau Bergmann and Lars going to take as a solution to the problem?

   Frau B.: _____

   _____

   Lars: _____

   _____

Fourth Part

You will now hear **four** news items taken from the radio, followed by the weather forecast. The news will be played **three** times; the first time right through, then in five segments with pauses, and finally right through again.

(Item 1)   CD3 Track 35

1. (i)   Why was the warning issued by the environmental organisation?

_____

_____

_____

(ii)   What items should be bought with caution?

_____

_____

_____

(Item 2)   CD3 Track 36

2. (i)   What are the main findings issued by the scientists?

_____

_____

_____

(ii)   What warning has been issued by the scientists?

_____

_____

_____

(Item 3)   CD3 Track 37

3. (i)   What conference took place in London, according to this item?

_____

_____

_____

(ii)   What is the German Minister for the Environment most concerned about?

_____

_____

_____

(Item 4)

CD3 Track 38

4. (i) What warning has been issued by the Department of the Environment? Give details.

_____

_____

_____

(ii) What effect will this have on drivers? Give details.

_____

_____

_____

(Item 5)

CD3 Track 39

5. Weather Forecast
(i) What kind of weather is expected today? Mention **three** details.

_____

_____

_____

(ii) What kind of weather is expected tonight? Give **three** details.

_____

_____

_____

Wortschatz

feiern – *to celebrate*
die Geburt Christi – *the birth of Christ*
die Weihnachtszeit – *Christmas time*
die Weihnachtskarte(-n) – *Christmas card*
Frohe Weihnachten! – *Happy Christmas!*
der Kuchen – *cake*
das Christkind – *Christ child*
der Weihnachtsmarkt(-märkte) – *Christmas fair*
der Nikolaus – *Santa*
der Weihnachtsmann – *Santa*
der Baum (Bäume) – *tree*
aufstellen – *to put up*
die (Weihnachts-)Gans – *goose*
der Truthahn – *turkey*
schmücken – *to decorate*
der Christbaumschmuck – *tree decorations*
das Geschenk(-e) – *present/gift*
der Lebkuchen – *gingerbread*
der Christstollen – *Christmas log*
der Glühwein – *mulled wine*
der Heiligabend – *Christmas Eve*
der Festbraten – *festive roast*
die Bescherung – *exchange of gifts*
die Kugel(-n) – *bauble*
die Kerze(-n) – *candle*
das Weihnachtslied(-er) – *Christmas hymn*

Test 19

German – Higher Level

LISTENING COMPREHENSION

First Part

CD3 Track 42

The interview will be played **three** times: first right through, then in segments with pauses, and finally right through again.

1. During what period does the *Nürnberger Christkindlesmarkt* take place?

   _____

   _____

2. List **four** items which can be bought at the *Christkindlesmarkt*.

   _____

   _____

   _____

   _____

3. Describe a speciality available at the *Christkindlesmarkt* that can be consumed while there.

   _____

   _____

4. How long has the *Nürnberger Christkindlesmarkt* been in existence?

   _____

5. Mention **three** places where a similar *Christkindlesmarkt* is held?

   _____

   _____

   _____

Second Part

CD3 Track 43

You will now hear a telephone conversation. The receptionist takes a message from the caller.

To allow you to answer **Question 1 (the note)**, the phonecall will be played **twice**, with a pause after each playing during which you should **fill in the box**. The phonecall will then be played for a third and final time to allow you to answer **Question 2** (the language of the phonecall).

1. Write out **in German** the note which the receptionist will leave.
   (**Key words, not full sentences**)
   The note should contain:
   - ■ to whom the caller wishes to pass on a message.
   - ■ name of caller.
   - ■ problem caller wishes to discuss.
   - ■ message regarding further contact (how, when).
   - ■ telephone number of caller.

Anruf für: _____

Anruf von: _____

Nachricht (stichwortartig):

Problem: _____

_____

Der Anrufer:

☐ ruft zurück.

☐ wartet auf Ihren sofortigen Rückruf.

☐ erbittet Besuch zu Hause.

☐ möchte einen Termin.

Telefonnummer des Anrufers: _____

Now answer Question 2.

2. After listening to the phonecall for the third time, pick out **three** examples of the language (**expressions and phrases, not tone of voice**) used by the caller that show the caller is **worried**.

_____

_____

_____

Third Part

CD3 Track 44

You will now hear a conversation between two people. The dialogue will be played **three** times, with a pause after each playing. Answer in English.

1. The conversation is between:
   (a) two teachers.
   (b) a principal and a pupil.
   (c) two pupils.
   (d) a pupil and a Religious Education teacher.

   Indicate your choice by putting **a, b, c** or **d** in the box provided. ☐

2. (i) Which adjective best describes Katja's attitude during the conversation?
   (a) indifferent
   (b) contented
   (c) annoyed
   (d) helpful

   Indicate your choice by putting **a, b, c** or **d** in the box provided. ☐

   (ii) Write down **two** details from the conversation to support your choice.

   _____

   _____

3. (i) Mention **three** details about Katja's parents.

   _____

   _____

   _____

   (ii) What suggestions do they make at the end of the conversation?

   _____

   _____

   _____

Fourth Part

You will now hear **four** news items taken from the radio, followed by the weather forecast. The news will be played **three** times; the first time right through, then in five segments with pauses, and finally right through again.

(Item 1)   `CD3 Track 45`

1. (i) Mention any **two** consequences of the house fires that happened over Christmas.

   _____

   _____

   (ii) What is thought to have caused the fire in Hamburg?

   _____

   _____

   _____

   _____

(Item 2)

2. (i) Which details reveal that the *Christkindlesmarkt* was a success?

_____

_____

_____

(ii) Mention any **two** details of the parade.

_____

_____

(Item 3)

3. (i) What kind of weather did Germany experience over the Christmas period?

_____

_____

_____

(ii) Mention any **two** consequences arising as a result of the weather conditions.

_____

_____

(Item 4)

4. Describe in note form how the police managed to catch a burglar in Zürich.

_____

_____

_____

_____

(Item 5)

5. Weather Forecast
   (i) What weather conditions are expected in Germany today?

_____

_____

(ii) What is the forecast for tomorrow?

_____

_____

_____

Test 20

German – Higher Level

LISTENING COMPREHENSION

First Part

CD3 Track 52

The interview will be played **three** times: first right through, then in segments with pauses, and finally right through again.

1. (i)   Why was Erika not able to contact Stefan?

    she lost her phone

    _____

    _____

    (ii) When was Erika due to meet the professor and what caused her to be delayed?

    her 2 – 4 for a test.

    _____

    _____

2. (i)   What was Erika to give to her professor?

a   project / test.

(ii) Why was it important that she handed it in today?

(she would) it was 20% of her grade

3. (i)   What proposal has Stefan for Erika? Give details.

(+2%) a house share.

(ii) Why is this opportunity only available until June?

4. Mention **three** costs associated with Stefan's proposal.

€240 , €30 per person each m-

5. (i)   From what date are they able to avail of the opportunity?

Next thursday.

(ii) What difficulty does Erika have with Stefan's proposal?

she can't pay her rent.

Second Part

You will now hear a telephone conversation. The receptionist takes a message from the caller.

To allow you to answer **Question 1 (the note)**, the phonecall will be played **twice**, with a pause after each playing during which you should **fill in the box**. The phonecall will then be played for a third and final time to allow you to answer **Question 2** (the **language** of the phonecall).

1. Write out **in German** the note which the receptionist will leave.
    (Key words, not full sentences)
    The note should contain:
    - ■ to whom the caller wishes to pass on a message.
    - ■ name of caller.
    - ■ problem caller wishes to discuss.
    - ■ message regarding further contact (how, when).
    - ■ telephone number of caller.

Name der Firma: _____

Anruf von: _____

Nachricht (stichwortartig):
Problem: _____

_____

Der Anrufer:
- ☐ ruft zurück.
- ☐ wartet auf Ihren sofortigen Rückruf.
- ☐ erbittet Besuch zu Hause.
- ☐ möchte einen Termin.

Telefonnummer des Anrufers: _____

Now answer Question 2.
2. After listening to the phonecall for the third time, pick out **three** examples of the language (**expressions and phrases, not tone of voice**) used by the caller that reveal the **nature of the business** the company is engaged in.

_____

_____

_____

Third Part

You will now hear a conversation between two people. The dialogue will be played **three** times, with a pause after each playing. Answer in English.

1. The conversation is between:
   (a) father and daughter.
   (b) a brother and sister.
   (c) a landlord and tenant.
   (d) two tenants.

   Indicate your choice by putting **a**, **b**, **c** or **d** in the box provided.   a

2. (i) Which adjective best describes the man's attitude to what the other person has to say?
   (a) indifferent
   (b) shocked
   (c) pleased
   (d) disappointed

   Indicate your choice by putting **a**, **b**, **c** or **d** in the box provided.   b.

   (ii) Write down **two** details from the conversation to support your choice.

   He just seems disappointed D is raising
   his voice He's trying to get her to stay.

3. (i) Why does Silke want to do what she says?

   She wants to be on her own
   and do what she wants.

   (ii) What decision do the two people come to at the end of the conversation? Give details.

   She is going too

Fourth Part

You will now hear **four** news items taken from the radio, followed by the weather forecast. The news will be played **three** times; the first time right through, then in five segments with pauses, and finally right through again.

(Item 1)   CD3 Track 55

1. Why was it so easy for the thieves to break into and rob the house in Braunschweig? Give **two** reasons.

_____

_____

(Item 2)   CD3 Track 56

2. Using plastic is a new design trend.
   (i)   What product is now made of plastic?

   _____

   _____

   (ii) Give **three** advantages mentioned for its use.

   _____

   _____

   _____

(Item 3)   CD3 Track 57

3. (i)   According to the bulletin, what is the cause of the disaster in northern California?

   _____

   _____

   _____

   _____

   (ii) Mention any **two** effects of the disaster.

   _____

   _____

(Item 4)

CD3 Track 58

4. (i) What kind of catastrophe was reported from Turkey?

_____

_____

_____

(ii) Give details of the damage caused.

_____

_____

_____

(Item 5)

CD3 Track 59

5. Weather Forecast
   (i) What kind of weather is expected:

   (a) for tomorrow? _____

   _____

   (b) for the weekend? _____

   _____

   (ii) What announcement is made at the end of the news? Give details.

   _____

   _____

   _____

Hörthemen

Vocabulary

Ordinary and Higher Levels

ADJEKTIVE

alt – neu/jung

altmodisch – modern

ängstlich – tapfer

arm – reich

aufgeregt – ruhig

besser – schlechter/schlimmer

best – schlechtest/schlimmst

billig – teuer

bitter – süß

blind – sehend

böse – gut

brav – unartig

breit – eng/schmal

un-deutlich

dick – dünn/schlank

doof – klug

dumm – intelligent

dunkel – hell

durstig – hungrig

un-eben

echt – falsch

un-ehrlich

einfach – kompliziert

ernst – heiter/lustig

falsch – richtig

faul – fleißig

un-fertig

fest – weich

feucht – trocken

flach – uneben/tief

un-freundlich

frisch – alt

froh – traurig/unglücklich

früh – spät

ganz – geteilt/kaputt

geizig – freigiebig/großzügig

un-genau

genug – mangelnd

gesund – krank/ungesund

glatt – rauh/uneben

un-gleich

glücklich – traurig/unglücklich

groß – klein

gut – schlecht

halb – voll

hart – weich

hässlich – hübsch/schön

heiß – kalt

hoch – niedrig/tief

un-höflich

hungrig – satt

interessant – langweilig

kindisch – erwachsen

un-klar

kräftig – schwach

kühl – mild

kurz – lang

lahm

langsam – schnell

launisch – ausgeglichen

laut – leise

lebendig – tot

leer – voll

lieb – frech/böse

mehr – weniger

un-möglich

müde – munter

nah – weit

nass – trocken

negativ – positiv

neidisch

nett – widerlich

neugierig – uninteressiert

normal – anormal

offen – geschlossen

öffentlich – privat

un-ordentlich _____
un-pünktlich _____
un-reif _____
riesig – winzig _____
un-ruhig _____
rund – eckig _____
salzig – ungesalzen _____
sauber – schmutzig _____
sauer – süß _____
un-scharf _____
schief – gerade _____
schläfrig – munter _____
schlau – dumm/dämlich

_____

schüchtern – selbstbewusst

_____

schwach – stark _____
un-sicher _____
streng – lässig _____
un-sympathisch _____
taub – hörend _____
viel – wenig _____
un-vorsichtig _____
wach – schlafend _____
wütend – gelassen _____
zornig – gelassen _____

ARBEIT
den Tisch abräumen _____
das Besteck abtrocknen

_____

Leute anrufen _____
die Wände anstreichen

_____

im Garten arbeiten _____
das Zimmer aufräumen

_____

Kuchen backen _____
basteln _____
Fleisch braten _____
bringen _____
Hemden bügeln _____
den Tisch decken _____
den Boden fegen _____
hämmern _____
kleben _____
Essen kochen _____
Sachen liefern _____
den Rasen mähen _____
Bilder malen _____

Blumen pflanzen _____
Fenster putzen _____
radieren _____
Holz sägen _____
Gemüse schälen _____
Emails schicken _____
Haare schneiden _____
Briefe schreiben _____
senden
Geschirr spülen _____
Staub saugen _____
telefonieren
Fehler unterstreichen _____
verbessern
Wäsche waschen _____
Karikaturen zeichnen _____

ARBEITSWELT
Angestellte(r)
arbeitslos _____
Arbeitsplatz _____
Arbeitsvertrag _____
Arbeitsweg _____
Arbeitszeiten _____
Ausbildung _____
Belegschaft _____
Betrieb
Betriebsferien _____
Bewerbungsbrief _____
Bezahlung _____
Chef/-in _____
Einkommenssteuer _____
Einstellung _____
Entlassung _____
Fabrik
Fähigkeit(en) _____
Firma (en) _____
Fließband
Gehalt _____
Geschäftsführer _____
Gewerkschaft _____
krank feiern _____
Krankenversicherung _____
Kündigung _____
Kurzarbeit _____
Lehrling _____
Lohn _____
Lohnerhöhung _____
Rentenversicherung _____
Rezession _____

Stellenangebot _____

Streik _____

Stress _____

Überstunden _____

AUTO

Auspuff _____

Autowerkstatt _____

das Auto springt nicht an

_____

Beifahrer _____

Benzin _____

Blinklicht _____

Bremsen _____

Fahrer _____

Fahrprüfung _____

Fahrzeug _____

Führerschein _____

Geschwindigkeit _____

Handbremse _____

Handschuhfach _____

Kennzeichen _____

Kofferraum _____

Kotflügel _____

Lastkraftwagen/Lkw _____

Lenkrad _____

Motor _____

Motorhaube _____

Nummernschild _____

Öl _____

Panne _____

Personenkraftwagen/Pkw

_____

Reifen _____

Reifenpanne _____

Rücksitz _____

Scheibenwischer _____

Sicherheitsgurt _____

Spiegel _____

Steuer _____

Stoßstange _____

Tankstelle _____

Tempolimit _____

Versicherung _____

Windschutzscheibe _____

AUTOUNFÄLLE

Auffahrunfall _____

Augenzeuge _____

Autoinsassen _____

defekte Bremsen _____

Fahrerflucht begehen _____

Glatteis _____

Massenkarambolage _____

Prellungen _____

Reisewelle _____

Rückreiseverkehr _____

Stau _____

Tote _____

Überholen _____

Verkehrskontrolle _____

Verletzte _____

zu schnelles Fahren _____

Zusammenstoß _____

Der Verkehr wurde lahmgelegt.

Die Straße wurde gesperrt.

_____

Ein Lastwagen ist verunglückt.

_____

Ein Geisterfahrer kam ihm entgegen.

_____

Ein Reifen ist geplatzt.

_____

Das Auto geriet in Brand.

_____

Das Auto kam ins Schleudern.

_____

Das Auto kam von der Straße ab.

_____

Das Auto prallte gegen einen Baum.

_____

Die Bremsen funktionierten
nicht/versagten. _____

Das Fahrzeug geriet ins Schleudern.

_____

Passagiere auf dem Rücksitz blieben
unverletzt. _____

Das Auto wurde aus der Kurve getragen.

_____

Der Pkw stieß mit einem
entgegenkommenden Fahrzeug
zusammen. _____

Der Beifahrer war nicht angeschnallt.

_____

Der Fahrer kam ums Leben.

_____

Der Fahrer wurde durch die Sonne
geblendet. _____

Der Fahrer stand unter Alkoholeinfluss.

_____

Die Fahrerin hat die Herrschaft/Kontrolle über das Auto verloren.

_____

Der Fahrer des Mofas trug keinen Helm.

_____

BERUFE

Arzt/Ärztin _____

Arbeiter(in) _____

Angestellte(r) _____

Architekt(in) _____

Auktionär(in) _____

Bankangestellte(r) _____

Beamte/Beamtin _____

Bauer/Bäuerin _____

Bäcker(in) _____

Bibliothekar(in) _____

Briefträger(in) _____

Buchhalter(in) _____

Buchhändler(in) _____

Bürgermeister(in) _____

Busschaffner(in) _____

Chef(in) _____

Chirurg(in) _____

Detektiv(in) _____

Dolmetscher(in) _____

Dozent(in) _____

Elektriker(in) _____

Fahrer(in) _____

Fahrlehrer(in) _____

Fotograf(in) _____

Frisör/Frisöse _____

Gärtner(in) _____

Geschäftsführer(in) _____

Hausmann/Hausfrau _____

Ingenieur _____

Journalist(in) _____

Kaufmann (pl. Kaufleute)

_____

Kellner(in) _____

Koch(Köchin) _____

Krankenpfleger(in) _____

Krankenschwester _____

Landwirt(in) _____

Lehrer(in) _____

Lehrling _____

Maler(in) _____

Mauerer(in) _____

Mechaniker(in) _____

Metzger(in) _____

Nonne _____

Pastor(in) _____

Pilot(in) _____

Polizist(in) _____

Postbote/Postbotin _____

Priester _____

Programmierer(in) _____

Reiseleiter(in) _____

Reporter(in) _____

Richter(in) _____

Schauspieler(in) _____

Schlosser _____

Schreiner(in) _____

Seemann(pl. Seeleute) _____

Sekretär(in) _____

Soldat(in) _____

Stenotypist(in) _____

Steward(ess) _____

Tierarzt/Tierärztin _____

Übersetzer(in) _____

Verkäufer(in) _____

Vertreter(in) _____

Zahnarzt/Zahnärztin _____

Zimmermann _____

Zollbeamter/Zollbeamtin

_____

Zugschaffner(in) _____

BUNDESLÄNDER

Baden-Württemberg _____

Bayern _____

Berlin _____

Brandenburg _____

Bremen _____

Hamburg _____

Hessen _____

Mecklenburg-Vorpommern

_____

Niedersachsen _____

Nordrhein-Westfalen _____

Rheinland-Pfalz _____

Saarland _____

Sachsen _____

Sachsen-Anhalt _____

Schleswig-Holstein _____

Thüringen _____

EINKÄUFE

Armbanduhr	_____
Bleistift(e)	_____
Briefmarke(n)	_____
Brot	_____
Brötchen	_____
Frischhaltefolie	_____
Gemüse	_____
Getränke	_____
Glühbirnen	_____
Handtuch(-tücher)	_____
Hefte	_____
Hemd	_____
Insektenspray	_____
Klopapier	_____
Knöpfe	_____
Küchenpapier	_____
Kugelschreiber(-)	_____
Nadel(n)	_____
Obst	_____
Ohrring	_____
Papierteller	_____
Parfüm	_____
Putzmittel	_____
Saft	_____
Schampoo	_____
Schnürsenkel(-)	_____
Schuhcreme	_____
Seife	_____
Spielzeug	_____
Sprudel	_____
Spülmittel	_____
Streichhölzer	_____
Süßigkeiten	_____
Taschentuch(-tücher)	_____
Uhr(en)	_____
Waschpulver	_____
Windeln	_____
Wolle	_____
Zahnpasta	_____

FÄCHER

Biologie	_____
Betriebswirtschaft(slehre)/BWL	
	_____
Chemie	_____
Deutsch	_____
Englisch	_____
Erdkunde	_____
Französisch	_____

Geographie	_____
Geschichte	_____
Hauswirtschaft	_____
Informatik	_____
Irisch	_____
Italienisch	_____
Kunst	_____
Mathe(matik)	_____
Physik	_____
Politik	_____
Russisch	_____
Spanisch	_____
Sport	_____
Technisches Zeichnen	_____
Werken	_____

FAMILIE

Adoptivkind	_____
Baby	_____
Bruder – Schwester	_____
Drilling	_____
Ehe – Scheidung	_____
(Ehe)frau – (Ehe)mann	
	_____
Ehepaar	_____
Eltern – Kind(er)	_____
Enkel – Enkelin	_____
Fünfling	_____
Geschwister – Einzelkind	
	_____
Kusine – Vetter	_____
Mutter – Vater	_____
Neffe – Nichte	_____
Oma – Opa	_____
Onkel – Tante	_____
Schwager – Schwägerin	
	_____
Schwiegermutter – Schwiegervater	
	_____
Sohn – Tochter	_____
Stiefmutter – Stiefvater	
	_____
Verlobte(r)	_____
Verwandte(r)	_____
Vierling	_____
Waisenkind	_____
Witwe	_____
Witwer	_____
Zwilling	_____
älter/jünger als ich	_____

der/die älteste – jüngste

_____

der/die zweitälteste _____
der/die drittjüngste _____
tot – lebendig/am Leben

_____

verwandt mit uns _____
verlobt mit _____
Meine Eltern sind geschieden.

_____

Meine Eltern leben getrennt.

_____

Mein Bruder/Meine Schwester ist
ledig/verheiratet. _____

FARBEN
beige _____
blaß _____
blau _____
bleich _____
braun _____
bunt _____
dunkel _____
gelb _____
grau _____
grün _____
hell _____
lila _____
orange _____
rosa _____
rot _____
schwarz _____
violett _____
weiß _____

FLEISCHSORTEN
Aufschnitt _____
Blutwurst _____
Bratwurst _____
Frikadelle _____
Gans _____
Gehacktes _____
Hähnchen _____
Hammelfleisch _____
Herz(en) _____
Huhn _____
Kalbsfleisch _____
Kotelett _____
Lammfleisch _____
Leber _____

Leberkäs _____
Pute _____
Rindfleisch _____
Schaschlik _____
Schinken _____
Schnitzel _____
Speck _____
Sülze _____
Truthahn _____
Wild _____
Wurst _____

GEBÄUDE
Apotheke(n) _____
Autowerkstatt(-stätte)

_____

Bäckerei(en) _____
Bahnhof(-höfe) _____
Bank(en) _____
Blumenladen(-läden) _____
Boutique(n) _____
Brücke(n) _____
Bücherei(en) _____
Buchhandlung(en) _____
Burg(en) _____
Büro(s) _____
Café(s) _____
Dom(e) _____
Dritte-Welt-Laden _____
Drogerie(n) _____
Einkaufszentrum(-zentren)

_____

Einwohnermeldeamt _____

Eisdiele(n) _____
Fabrik(en) _____
Feinkostladen(-läden) _____
Fleischerei(en) _____
Flughafen(-häfen) _____
Freibad(-bäder) _____
Frisörsalon(s) _____
Fundbüro(s) _____
Garage(n) _____
Gefängnis(-se) _____
Geschenkartikelladen(-läden)

Gymnasium(-ien) _____
Hallenbad(-bäder) _____
Heimatmuseum(-een) _____

Heimwerkergeschäft(e)
_____

Imbisskiosk(e) _____
Imbissstube(n) _____
Jugendherberge(n) _____
Juwelier(e) _____
Kathedrale(n) _____
Kaufhaus(-häuser) _____
Kino(s) _____
Kirche(n) _____
Kneipe(n) _____
Konditorei(en) _____
Krankenhaus(-häuser)
_____

Kunstgalerie(n) _____
Kunstgewerbeladen(-läden)
_____

Metzgerei(en) _____
Möbelgeschäft(e) _____
Parkhaus(-häuser) _____
Pension(en) _____
Pizzeria(-ien) _____
Polizeiwache(n) _____
Postamt(-ämter) _____
Rathaus(-häuser) _____
Reformhaus(-häuser)
_____

Reinigung _____
Reisebüro(s) _____
Restaurant(s) _____
Scheune(n) _____
Schloss(Schlösser) _____
Schreibwarenladen(-läden)
_____

Schuhgeschäft(e) _____
Schule(n) _____
Schuppen(-) _____
Sparkasse(n) _____
Spielwarenladen(-läden)
_____

Stadion(-ien) _____
Tankstelle(n) _____
Tierladen(-läden) _____
Turnhalle(n) _____
Universität(en) _____
Verkehrsamt(-ämter) _____
Wäscherei(en) _____
Wechselstube(n) _____
Werkstatt(-stätte) _____
Wirtschaft(en) _____

GEFÜHLE
Angst/ängstlich _____
Ärger/ärgerlich _____
Eifersucht/eifersüchtig

Einsamkeit/einsam _____
Eitelkeit/ eitel _____
Enttäuschung/enttäuscht
_____

Feindseligkeit/feindselig
_____

Freude/froh _____
Freundlichkeit/freundlich

Glück/glücklich _____
Güte/gut _____
Hass/gehässig _____
Hoffnung/hoffnungsvoll
_____

Laune/launisch (gut/schlecht gelaunt)

Liebe/liebevoll _____
Neid/neidisch _____
Nervosität/nervös _____
Neugier/neugierig _____
Optimismus/optimistisch
_____

Pessimismus/pessimistisch
_____

Schüchternheit/schüchtern

Stolz/stolz _____
Trauer/traurig _____
Wut/wütend _____
Zorn/zornig _____

GEHEN
zu Hause ankommen _____
aus dem Zug aussteigen
_____

nach Hause eilen _____
ins Auto einsteigen _____
schnell gehen _____
hetzen _____
hüpfen _____
nach Hause kommen _____
kriechen _____
laufen _____
rasen _____
reisen _____

rennen _____
sausen _____
schleichen _____
schlürfen _____
sich beeilen _____
sich bewegen _____
sich entfernen _____
sich verlaufen _____
spazierengehen _____
springen _____
steigen _____
stolpern _____
stürzen _____
überqueren _____
wandern _____

GEMÜSE

Blumenkohl _____
Bohne(n) _____
Broccoli _____
Erbse(n) _____
Gurke(n) _____
Karotte(n) _____
Kartoffel(n) _____
Knoblauch _____
Kohl _____
Kopfsalat _____
Lauch _____
Mais _____
Möhre(n) _____
Mohrrübe(n) _____
Pabrikaschote(n) _____
Pastinake(n) _____
Pilz(e) _____
Radieschen _____
Rosenkohl _____
Rote Beete _____
Schlangengurke(n) _____
Sellerie _____
Spinat _____
Steckrübe(n) _____
Tomate(n) _____
Zwiebel(n) _____

GEOGRAPHIE

Ahr _____
Allgäu _____
Alpen _____
Bayerischer Wald _____
Bodensee _____

Donau _____
Elbe _____
Genf _____
Harz _____
Isar _____
Kontinent _____
Main _____
Mittelgebirge _____
Mittelmeer _____
Mosel _____
Nordsee _____
Oder _____
Ostfriesische Inseln _____
Ostfriesland _____
Ostsee _____
Ozean _____
Rhein _____
Ruhr _____
Ruhrgebiet _____
Schwarzwald _____
Taunus _____
Weser _____
Wien _____

GESELLSCHAFT

Abtreibung _____
Alkoholismus _____
Arbeitslosenquote _____
Arbeitslosigkeit _____
Armut _____
Ausländerfeindlichkeit
_____
Ausreißer _____
Aussetzung _____
Benachteiligung _____
beschädigen _____
Bombenanschlag _____
Brandstiftung _____
Desinteresse _____
Diebstahl _____
Diskriminierung _____
Dritte Welt _____
Drogen _____
Drogenhandel _____
Dürre _____
Einbrecher _____
Einbruch _____
Einsamkeit _____
Entfremdung _____
Flaute _____

Flüchtling _____

Frieden _____

Geiseln _____

Geiselnahme _____

Geistig behindert _____

Gewalt _____

Heroin _____

Hunger _____

Hungersnot _____

Inflation _____

Jugendbanden _____

karitative Organisation(en)

_____

Kinderschänder _____

Kindesmisshandlung _____

Komasaufen _____

Körperbehinderung _____

Kredithaie _____

Krieg _____

Kriminalität _____

Langzeitarbeitslose _____

Massenschlägerei _____

Mobbing _____

Mord _____

Obdachlose _____

Obdachlosigkeit _____

Öffentlichkeit _____

Opfer _____

Passivrauchen _____

Perspektivelosigkeit _____

Preiserhöhung _____

Prostitution _____

Prügelei _____

Rassismus _____

Raubüberfall _____

Rauchverbot _____

Rauschgift _____

Rechtsradikale _____

Rentner _____

Rezession _____

Rinderwahn _____

(Ungewollte) Schwangerschaft

_____

Schwarzmarkt _____

Schweingrippe _____

Schwindel _____

Sekte _____

Selbstmord _____

Slums _____

Spätaussiedler _____

Spenden _____

Straftaten _____

Streit _____

Stress _____

Sucht _____

Süchtige(r) _____

Täter _____

Totschlag _____

Überfall _____

Verbraucher _____

Verbrechen _____

Verbrecher _____

Verdächtige _____

Vergewaltigung _____

Verhütungsmittel _____

Verzweiflung _____

Vorurteil(e) _____

GESUNDHEIT

Ausschlag _____

Beinbruch _____

Blinddarmentzündung

_____

Durchfall _____

Erkältung _____

Fieber _____

Gelbsucht _____

Gips _____

Grippe _____

Halsschmerzen _____

Herzanfall _____

Heuschnupfen _____

Hirnschlag _____

Husten _____

Keuchhusten _____

Kopfschmerzen _____

Krebs _____

Lebensmittelvergiftung

_____

Leukämie _____

Lungenentzündung _____

Magengeschwür _____

Mandelentzündung _____

Masern _____

Mittelohrentzündung

_____

Nähte _____

Ohrenschmerzen _____

Schnupfen _____

Schweinegrippe _____

Sonnenbrand	_____	
Sonnenstich	_____	
Spritze	_____	
Windpocken	_____	
Zahnschmerzen	_____	
Ziegenpeter/mumps	_____	
Zuckerkrankheit	_____	

GETRÄNKE

Alsterwasser	_____
Apfelsaft	_____
Bier	_____
Cola	_____
Fruchtsaft	_____
Heiße Schokolade	_____
Kaffee	_____
Kakao	_____
Limonade	_____
Milch	_____
Mineralwasser	_____
Orangensaft	_____
Radler	_____
Saft (Säfte)	_____
Schnaps	_____
Sprudel	_____
Tee	_____
Tomatensaft	_____
Wasser	_____
Wein	_____
Whisky	_____

DAS HAUS

Badezimmer(-)	_____
Balkon(s)	_____
Besitzer	_____
Bungalow(s)	_____
Dach(¨er)	_____
Decke(n)	_____
Diele(n)	_____
Einfamilienhaus(-häuser)	
	_____
Erdgeschoss(sse)	_____
Esszimmer(-)	_____
Fenster(-)	_____
Flur(e)	_____
Fußboden(¨)	_____
Gang(¨e)	_____
Garage(n)	_____
Gardine(n)	_____
Garten(¨)	_____

Gästezimmer(-)	_____
Gewächshaus	_____
Hausmeister(-)	_____
Hausordnung	_____
Kamin(e)	_____
Keller(-)	_____
Kinderzimmer(-)	_____
Klingel(n)	_____
Küche(n)	_____
Miete	_____
Mieter(-)	_____
Möbel	_____
Nachbar(n)	_____
Obstgarten(-gärten)	_____
Rasen(-)	_____
Reihenhaus(¨er)	_____
Schlafzimmer(-)	_____
Schornstein(e)	_____
Stock (¨e)	_____
Stockwerk(e)	_____
Teppich(e)	_____
Toilette(n)	_____
Treppe(n)	_____
Tür(en)	_____
Vermieter(-)	_____
Wand(¨e)	_____
Wohnblock(-blöcke)	_____
Wohnung(en)	_____
Wohnzimmer(-)	_____
Zaun(Zäune)	_____
Wir haben drei Zimmer unten/oben	
	_____
Der Garten ist hinten/vorn	
	_____

HAUS: GERÄTE

Backofen(öfen)	_____
Bügeleisen(-)	_____
CD-Spieler(-)	_____
Computer(-)	_____
Fernseher(-)	_____
Gasofen(-öfen)	_____
Herd(e)	_____
Hifi-Turm(-türme)	_____
Kassettenspieler(-)	_____
Kessel(-)	_____
Kühlschrank(-schränke)	
	_____
Mikrowellengerät(e)	_____
Lampe(-n)	

Plattenspieler(-) _____

Radio(s) _____

Spülmaschine(n) _____

Staubsauger(-) _____

Stereoanlage(n) _____

Telefon(e) _____

Tiefkühltruhe(n) _____

Videorecorder(-) _____

Wäschetrockner(-) _____

Waschmaschine(n) _____

HOBBYS

Angeln _____

Archäologie _____

Astronomie _____

Backen _____

Basketball _____

Basteln _____

Bergsteigen _____

Briefeschreiben _____

Briefmarken sammeln

_____

Computer _____

Dame _____

Diskutieren _____

Federball _____

Fernsehen _____

Flugzeugmodelle _____

Fremdsprachen _____

Fußball _____

Geschichte _____

Insekten _____

Jogging _____

Karten _____

Kochen _____

Korbball _____

Laufen _____

Leichtathletik _____

Lesen _____

Malen _____

Münzen sammeln _____

Musik _____

Nähen _____

Puppen _____

Puzzeln _____

Quizze _____

Radfahren _____

Reiten _____

Schach _____

Segeln _____

Schilaufen _____

Sport _____

Stricken _____

Tanzen _____

Tischtennis _____

Wandern _____

Wasserschi _____

Zeichnen _____

IM KAUFHAUS

Alles fürs Bad _____

Antiquitäten _____

Autozubehör _____

Babybekleidung _____

Beistellmöbel _____

Beleuchtung _____

Bettwaren _____

Bilder _____

Boutique _____

Bücher _____

Bürotechnik _____

Damenbademoden _____

Damenhüte _____

Damenoberbekleidung

_____

Damenwäsche _____

Elektrogeräte _____

Erdgeschoss _____

Fernsehen _____

Foto _____

Gardinen _____

Geschenkartikel _____

Glas _____

Handarbeiten _____

Handschuhe _____

Handys _____

Haushaltswaren _____

Heimwerker _____

Herrenartikel _____

Herrenoberbekleidung

_____

Interiör _____

Kinderbekleidung _____

Kreditbüro _____

Kundendienst _____

Lebensmittel _____

Lederwaren _____

Möbel _____

Modewaren _____

Obergeschoss	_____	**KLEIDUNG**	
Optik	_____	Anorak	_____
Parfümerie	_____	Anzug(-züge)	_____
Pelze	_____	Ärmel(-)	_____
Porzellan	_____	Badeanzug(-züge)	
Reisebüro	_____	Bademantel(-mäntel)	_____
Rundfunk	_____	Baumwolle	_____
Schallplatten	_____	Bikini(s)	_____
Schirme	_____	Bluse(n)	_____
Schmuck	_____	Büstenhalter(-)	_____
Schnellrestaurant	_____	Größe(n)	_____
Schreibwaren	_____	Gummistiefel	
Schuhe	_____	Gürtel(-)	
Stoffe	_____	Handschuh(e)	_____
Strümpfe	_____	Handtuch(-tücher)	_____
Süßwaren	_____	Hemd(en)	_____
Tabakwaren	_____	Höschen(-)	_____
Teppiche	_____	Hose(n)	_____
Tischtücher	_____	Hosenträger(-)	_____
Uhren	_____	Hut("e)	_____
Untergeschoss	_____	Jacke(n)	_____
Versicherungen	_____	Jeans	_____
Zeitschriften	_____	Kleid(er)	_____
Zeitungen	_____	Knopf("e)	_____
		Kostüm	_____
		Kragen(-)	_____
KATASTROFEN		Krawatte(n)	_____
Bergwerksunglück	_____	Leder	_____
Bombenanschlag	_____	Mantel(¨)	_____
Dürre	_____	Mütze(n)	_____
Eisenbahnunglück	_____	Nachthemd(en)	_____
Erdbeben	_____	Pantoffel(n)	_____
Erdrutsch	_____	Pullover(-)	_____
Flugzeugabsturz	_____	Regenmantel(-mäntel)	
Hochwasser	_____		_____
Hungersnot	_____	Reißverschluss(-üsse)	_____
Krieg	_____	Rock("e)	_____
Lawine	_____	Sandale(n)	_____
Massaker	_____	Schal(s)	_____
Minenunglück	_____	Schlafanzug(-anzüge)	
Orkan	_____		_____
Sturm	_____	Schlips(e)	_____
Taifun	_____	Schnürsenkel(-)	_____
Überschwemmungen		Schuh(e)	_____
	_____	Slip(s)	_____
Unwetter	_____	Stiefel(-)	_____
Vulkanausbruch	_____	Strickjacke(n)	_____
Waldbrand	_____	Strumpf("e)	_____
Wirbelsturm	_____	Strumpfhose(n)	_____
Zug entgleist	_____	Tasche(n)	_____

Taschentuch(-tücher) _____
Top _____
Trainingsanzug(-züge)

_____
Unterhemd(en) _____
Unterhose(n) _____
Unterrock(-röcke) _____
Weste(n) _____
Wolle _____

DER KÖRPER
Arm(e) (Oberarm/Unterarm)

_____
Auge(n) _____
Augenbraue(n) _____
Bart _____
Bauch _____
Bein(e) _____
Blinddarm _____
Blut _____
Brust(¨e) _____
Daumen(-) _____
Ellenbogen(-) _____
Ferse(n) _____
Finger(-) _____
Fuß(¨e) _____
Fußgelenk(e) _____
Gesicht(er) _____
Gesäß(e) _____
Haar(e) _____
Hals(Hälse) _____
Hand(¨e) _____
Handfläche(n) _____
Handgelenk(e) _____
Haut _____
Herz(en) _____
Hintern(-) _____
Hüfte(n) _____
Kehle _____
Kinn _____
Knie(-) _____
Knochen(-) _____
Kopf(¨e) _____
Lippe(n) _____
Magen _____
Mandeln _____
Mund _____
Muskel(n) _____
Nacken _____
Nagel(¨) _____

Nase(n) _____
Nerv(en) _____
Niere(-n) _____
Ohr(en) _____
Pickel(-) _____
Rippe(n) _____
Rücken(-) _____
Schenkel(-) _____
Schulter(n) _____
Stirn _____
Taille(-) _____
Vene(n) _____
Wade(n) _____
Wange(n) _____
Zahn (Zähne) _____
Zeh(e) _____
Zeigefinger(-) _____
Zunge(n) _____

LANDSCHAFT
Bach(Bäche) _____
Baum(Bäume) _____
Berg(e) _____
Bergspitze(n) _____
Blatt(¨er) _____
Blume(n) _____
Busch(¨e) _____
Feld(er) _____
Felsen(-) _____
Fluss(Flüsse) _____
Gebirge _____
Gebüsch _____
Gras _____
Hecke(n) _____
Heide(n) _____
Hügel(-) _____
Insel(n) _____
Klippe(n) _____
Küste(n) _____
Laub _____
Moor(e) _____
See(n)(der) _____
See(n)(die) _____
Steinmauer(n) _____
Strand(¨e) _____
Sumpf(¨e) _____
Tal(Täler) _____
Ufer(-) _____
Wald(¨er) _____
Wasserfall(-fälle) _____

Welle	_____	Salz	_____
Wiese(n)	_____	Schinken	_____
Wüste(n)	_____	Schokolade	_____
		Senf	_____
		Spaghetti	_____
		Sprudel	_____

LEBENSMITTEL

Apfelsaft	_____	Suppe	_____
Bier	_____	Tee	_____
Brötchen	_____	Wasser	_____
Backpulver	_____	Wein	_____
Butter	_____	Wurst	_____
Chips	_____	Zucker	_____
Ei(er)	_____	Zwiebeln	_____
Eis	_____		
Essig	_____		

LESESTOFF

Fisch	_____	Abenteuerroman(e)	_____
Fischstäbchen(-)	_____	Archäologiebuch(-bücher)	
Fleisch	_____		_____
Fruchtsaft	_____	Astronomiebuch(-bücher)	
Gemüse	_____		_____
Gewürz(e)	_____	Autobiografie(n)	_____
Honig	_____	Biografie(n)	_____
Huhn	_____	Erzählung(en)	_____
Jogurt	_____	Gedicht(e)	_____
Kaffee	_____	Geschichtsbuch(-bücher)	
Kakao	_____		_____
Käse	_____	Humor	_____
Kekse	_____	Illustrierte	_____
Knäckebrot	_____	Jugendbuch(-bücher)	
Kotelett	_____		_____
Kuchen	_____	Kinderbuch(-bücher)	_____
Limonade	_____	Klassiker(-)	_____
Linsen	_____	Krimi(s)	_____
Margarine	_____	Kurzgeschichte(n)	_____
Marmelade	_____	Legende(n)	_____
Mehl	_____	Liebesroman(e)	_____
Milch	_____	Lyrik	_____
Nudeln	_____	Magazin(e)	_____
Obst	_____	Märchen(-)	_____
Öl	_____	Reisebeschreibung(en)	
Olivenöl	_____		_____
Orangensaft	_____	Roman(e)	_____
Pfeffer	_____	Sachbuch(-bücher)	_____
Plätzchen	_____	Sage(n)	_____
Pudding	_____	Science-Fiction	_____
Reis	_____	Sportbuch(-bücher)	_____
Rindfleisch	_____	Tierbuch(-bücher)	_____
Rosinen	_____	Übersetzung(en)	_____
Saft	_____	Zeitschrift(en)	_____
Sahne	_____	Zeitung(en)	_____

MÖBEL
Bank(¨e) _____
Bett(en) _____
Bücherregal(e) _____
Computertisch(e) _____
Couch(en) _____
Hocker(-) _____
Kleiderschrank(-schränke)
_____
Kommode(n) _____
Küchenschrank(-schränke)
_____
Liegesessel(-) _____
Nachttisch(e) _____
Regal(e) _____
Rolltisch(e) _____
Schreibtisch(e) _____
Schublade(n) _____
Sekretär(e) _____
Servierwagen(-) _____
Sessel(–) _____
Sofa(s) _____
Spiegel(-) _____
Spiegelschrank(-schränke)
_____
Stehlampe(n) _____
Stöckelbett(en) _____
Stuhl(¨e) _____
Teewagen(-) _____
Tisch(e) _____
Vitrine(n) _____

OBST
Ananas(-sse) _____
Apfel(¨) _____
Apfelsine(n) _____
Aprikose(n) _____
Banane(n) _____
Beere(n) _____
Birne(n) _____
Erdbeere(n) _____
Haselnuss(-nüsse) _____
Himbeere(n) _____
Kirsche(n) _____
Kokosnuss(-nüsse) _____
Melone(n) _____
Nuss(Nüsse) _____
Pampelmuse(n) _____
Pfirsich(e) _____
Pflaume(n) _____

Rhabarber _____
Stachelbeere(n) _____
Traube(n) _____
Zitrone(n) _____

POLITISCHE PARTEIEN
Find out what the following stand for.
CDU _____
CSU _____
Die Grünen _____
Die Linke _____
FDP _____
KPD _____
NPD _____
Republikaner _____
SPD _____

POLITIK
Abgeordnete(r) _____
Abstimmung _____
Bundeskanzler/-in _____
Bundesrat _____
Bundestag _____
Fünfprozentklausel _____
Koalition _____
Landtag _____
Mandat _____
Mehrheit _____
Minderheit _____
Ministerium _____
Opposition _____
Parlament _____
Partei _____
Politik _____
Politiker _____
Stichwahl _____
Stimme _____
Wahl _____
Wähler _____
Wahlkreis _____

REISEN
Andenken _____
Aussteigen/einsteigen
_____
Ausstellung _____
Bahnhof(-höfe) _____
Bahnsteig _____
besichtigen _____
Fest(e) _____

fliegen _____
Flughafen(-häfen) _____
Gleis(e) _____
Grenze _____
Karte(n) _____
Koffer(-) _____
Kultur _____
Landen _____
packen / auspacken _____
Schaffner(-) _____
Souvenir(s) _____
tanken _____
umsteigen _____
Veranstaltung(en) _____
verzollen _____
Zoll _____

SCHULE 1

Fachhochschule(n) _____
Gesamtschule(n) _____
Grundschule(n) _____
Gymnasium(-asien) _____
Hauptschule(n) _____
Hochschule(n) _____
Kindergarten(-gärten) _____

Realschule(n) _____
Universität(en) _____

SCHULE 2

Arbeit(en) _____
benoten _____
Blauer Brief _____
Bleistift(e) _____
Buch(¨er) _____
Buntstift(e) _____
Ergebnisse _____
Etui(s) _____
Examen(Examina) _____
Federtasche(n) _____
Filzstift(e) _____
Füller(-) _____
Globus(Globen) _____
Heft(e) _____
Kalender(-) _____
Klassenbuch _____
Klassensprecher/-in _____
Klassenlehrer/-in _____
Klausur(-en) _____
Klebstoff _____

Kollegium _____
Kreide _____
Kugelschreiber(-) _____
Landkarte(n) _____
Lehrer(-) _____
Lehrerin(nen) _____
Lehrerzimmer(-) _____
Leistung(en) _____
lernen _____
Lineal(e) _____
Mittlere Reife _____
Note(n) _____
Notizblock(-blöcke) _____
Papier(e) _____
Papierkorb(-körbe) _____
pauken _____
Pause(n) _____
Pinsel(-) _____
Prüfung(en) _____
Pult(e) _____
Radiergummi(s) _____
Raucherecke _____
Realschulabschluss _____
Rechnen _____
Rektor(en) _____
Schere(n) _____
Schüler(-) _____
Schulhalbjahr(e) _____
Schulhof(-höfe) _____
Schulleiter(-) _____
Schultasche(n) _____
Stundenplan(-pläne) _____
Tadel _____
Tafel(n) _____
Taschenrechner _____
Tornister(–) _____
Türklinke(n) _____
Unterricht _____
Versetzung _____
Wand(¨e) _____
Zeichnung(en) _____
Zeugnis(se) _____

SCHULE 3

Alphabet(e) _____
Abitur _____
Aufsatz(-sätze) _____
Buchstabe(n) _____
Diktat(e) _____
Gedicht(e) _____

Grammatik _____

Kapitel _____

Komma(s) _____

Projekt(e) _____

Punkt(e) _____

Rechtschreibung _____

Referat(e) _____

Regel(n) _____

Satz(Sätze) _____

Strafarbeit _____

Übung(en) _____

Wort(e or ¨er) _____

Wörterbuch(¨er) _____

SCHULE 4

Ich besuche ein Gymnasium.

_____

Ich gehe (nicht) gern in die Schule.

_____

Ich muss sitzenbleiben.

_____

Ich habe die Prüfung bestanden.

_____

Ich bin durchgefallen.

_____

Ich hatte eine Fünf in Deutsch.

_____

Ich finde Mathe schwierig/leicht.

_____

Der Unterricht ist ganz interessant/
langweilig. _____

Herr Müller gibt Französisch.

_____

Wir haben eine Doppelstunde Chemie.

_____

Mein Bruder macht sein Abitur.

_____

Die Deutschstunde fällt aus.

_____

Der Lehrer gibt zu viel auf.

_____

Mein Lieblingsfach ist Kunst.

_____

Meine Lieblingsfächer sind Deutsch
und Musik. _____

SEE/MEER

Badeanzug(-züge) _____

Boot(e) _____

Bootsfahrt(en) _____

Düne(n) _____

Eimer(–) _____

Hafen(¨) _____

Insel(n) _____

Klippe(n) _____

Liegestuhl(¨e) _____

Motorboot(e) _____

Möwe(n) _____

Muschel(n) _____

Ruderboot(e) _____

Sandburg(en) _____

Seetang _____

Segelboot(e) _____

Sonnenhut(¨e) _____

Sonnenschirm(e) _____

Spaten(–) _____

Strand(¨e) _____

Wasserschi _____

Wattwanderung(en) _____

Welle(n) _____

SPORT

Angeln _____

Autorennen _____

Bergsteigen _____

Billiard _____

Bobfahren _____

Bowling _____

Boxen _____

Brennball _____

Fallschirmspringen _____

Fechten _____

Fußball _____

Golf _____

Handball _____

Hochsprung _____

Jagd/Jagen _____

Judo _____

Kegeln _____

Korbball _____

Leichathletik _____

Pferderennen _____

Querfeldeinlaufen _____

Radsport _____

Reiten _____

Ringen _____

Rodeln _____

Schwimmen _____

Segeln _____

Schilaufen _____

Springreiten	_____
Surfen	_____
Tauchen	_____
Tennis	_____
Tischtennis	_____
Turnen	_____
Volleyball	_____
Wasserball	_____
Wasserschi	_____
Weitsprung	_____
Windhundrennen	_____
Windsurfen	_____

TIERE/TIERVERGLEICHE

Affe(n)	_____
Stark wie ein Bär(en)	_____
Dachs(e)	_____
Dinosaurier(-)	_____
Eichhörnchen(-)	_____
Wie ein Elefant(en) im Przellanladen	_____
Ente(n)	_____
stur wie Esel(-)	_____
schlau wie ein Fuchs(¨e)	_____
du dumme Gans(¨e)!	_____
Giraffe(n)	_____
Goldfisch(e)	_____
Hamster(-)	_____
Hase(n)/Angsthase	_____
Huhn(¨er)	_____
Hund(e)	_____
Igel(-)	_____
Kalb(¨er)	_____
Käfer(–)	_____
Kamel(e)	_____
Kanarienvogel(¨)	_____
Känguru(s)	_____
Kaninchen(-)	_____
Katze(n)	_____
Krokodil(e)	_____
dumme Kuh(¨e)	_____
Lamm(¨er)	_____
Löwe(n)	_____
still wie eine Maus(¨e)	_____
Meerschweinchen(-)	_____
Otter(–)	_____
Papagei(en)	_____
Pferd(e)	_____
Ratte(n)/Leseratte	_____

Schaf(e)	_____
Schildkröte(n)	_____
Schlange(n)	_____
Schmetterling(e)	_____
Dreckigwie ein Schwein(e)	_____
Spinne(n)	_____
Tiger(-)	_____
Vogel(¨)	_____
Wellensittich(e)	_____
Wurm(¨er)	_____
Zebra(s)	_____
Ziege(n)	_____

TRANSPORT

Auto(s)	_____
Boot(e)	_____
Bus(se)	_____
Dreirad(-räder)	_____
Fähre(n)	_____
Fahrrad(-räder)	_____
Flugzeug(e)	_____
Hubschrauber(-)	_____
Jacht(en)	_____
Lastwagen(-)/Lkw	_____
Luftkissenboot(e)	_____
Mofa(s)	_____
Moped(s)	_____
Motorrad	_____
Rakete(n)	_____
Raumschiff(e)	_____
Ruderboot(e)	_____
S-Bahn(en)	_____
Schiff(e)	_____
Straßenbahn(en)	_____
Taxi(s)	_____
Traktor	_____
Trecker(-)	_____
U-Bahn(en)	_____
U-Boot(e)	_____
Wagen(-)	_____
Zug(¨e)	_____

UMWELT

Autoabgase	_____
Beton	_____
Chemikalien	_____
Düngemittel	_____
Getränkedosen	_____
Gift	_____

giftige Substanzen _____
Grundwasser _____
Industrieabfall _____
Industrieanlagen _____
Kartons _____
Lösemittel _____
Luftverschmutzung _____
Müll _____
Müllbeseitigung _____
Mülleimer _____
Müllentsorgung _____
Müllhalde _____
Müllverbrennungsanlage
_____

Naturschutz _____
Ozonschicht _____
Rauch _____
Recycling _____
Reinigungsmittel _____
Saurer Regen
Schadstoff _____
Smog _____
Spray _____
Verbrennungsanlage _____
Verpackung _____
Verseuchtes Wasser _____
Waldsterben _____
Zubetonierung _____

WETTER
Aufheiterung(en) _____
Blitz(e) _____
Brise(n) _____
Donner _____
Eis _____
Frost("e) _____
Frühnebel _____
Gefrierpunkt _____
Gewitter(-) _____
Glatteis _____
Null Grad _____
Hagel _____
Hagelkorn-(körner) _____
Himmel _____
Hitzewelle(n) _____
Hoch _____
Jahreszeit(en) _____
Kälte _____
Mond _____
Nebel _____

Niederschlag("e) _____
Nieselregen _____
Orkan(e) _____
Regen _____
Schauer(-) _____
einzelne Schauer _____
vereinzelte Schauer _____
Schnee _____
Schneeregen _____
Sonne _____
Sonnenschein _____
Sturm("e) _____
Taifun _____
Temperatur(en) _____
Tief _____
Wärme _____
Wetterbericht(e) _____
Wettervorhersage(n) _____
Wirbelsturm(-stürme)
_____

Wolke(n) _____
Wolkenbruch(-brüche)
_____

eine geschlossene Wolkendecke
_____

bedeckt _____
bewölkt _____
dichter Nebel
diesig _____
frisch _____
frostig
gelegentlich Regen _____
heiß _____
heiter _____
kalt
kühl _____
mäßig _____
mild _____
nebelig
niederschlagsfrei
örtlich Gewitter _____
regnerisch _____
schwül _____
sturmartige Winde _____
stürmisch _____
trocken
verbreitet Nebel _____
warm _____
windig _____
wolkig _____

zeitweise Regen _____
zunächst sonnig _____
zunehmend sonnig _____
Es regnet in Strömen. _____
Es schneit _____
Der Himmel zieht sich zu.

_____
Es donnert und blitzt. _____
Es ist mir zu heiß/kalt.

_____
Es gießt _____
Wie wird das Wetter morgen?

_____

ZEITEN

Abend _____
Abenddämmerung _____
Augenblick(e) _____
Frühling _____
Herbst _____
Jahr(e) _____
Jahreszeit(en) _____
Jahrhundert(e) _____
Jahrtausend(e) _____
Jahrzehnt(e) _____
Minute(n) _____
Mittag _____
Mitternacht _____
Moment(e) _____
Monat(e) _____
Morgen _____
Morgendämmerung _____
Nachmittag _____
Nacht _____
Sekunde(n) _____
Sommer _____
Stunde(n) _____
jeden Tag(e) _____
den ganzen Tag _____
Uhrzeit _____
Vormittag _____
Winter _____
Woche(n) _____
Wochenende _____

ZEITADVERBIEN

abends _____
bald _____
bisher _____
damals _____

danach _____
dann _____
davor _____
früh _____
früher _____
gestern _____
heute _____
heute Morgen _____
heute Nachmittag
heute Abend _____
heute Nacht _____
immer _____
jährlich _____
jemals _____
jetzt _____
mittags _____
morgen _____
morgen früh _____
morgens _____
nachher _____
nachmittags _____
nachts _____
neulich _____
nie _____
(immer) noch _____
nun _____
plötzlich _____
pünktlich _____
rechtzeitig _____
sekundenlang _____
spät _____
später _____
spätestens _____
stündlich _____
täglich _____
übermorgen _____
verspätet _____
vorgestern _____
vorher _____
vormittags _____
wöchentlich _____
zeitweise _____

MUSIKINSTRUMENTE

Akkordeon _____
Banjo _____
Blechflöte _____
Dudelsack _____
Flöte _____
Geige _____

Gitarre   _____

Harfe   _____

Klavier   _____

Klarinette   _____

Mundharmonika   _____

Mundorgel   _____

Orgel   _____

Rekorder   _____

Trommel   _____

Notizen